SAVE

Other titles by

Shannon Lush and Jennifer Fleming

Spotless

Speedcleaning

How to be Comfy

SHANNON LUSH & JENNIFER FLEMING

SAVE

Your **money**, your **time**, your **planet**

Inspired
uses for
common
household
items

ABC
Books

Published by ABC Books for the
AUSTRALIAN BROADCASTING CORPORATION
GPO Box 9994 Sydney NSW 2001

National Library of Australia
Cataloguing-in-Publication entry

Lush, Shannon.

Save : your money, your time, your planet / Shannon Lush,
Jennifer Fleming.

1st ed.

ISBN 9780733324444 (pbk.)

Includes index.

1. House furnishings. interior decoration. Salvage (Waste, etc.)
I. Fleming Jennifer. II. Australian Broadcasting Corporation.

Fleming, Jennifer.
Australian Broadcasting Corporation.

645

Designed and typeset by saso content & design pty ltd
Illustrations by Alan Laver
Internal photography by Rick Lush
  (except pages 52–3, photograph by Sergej Razvodorski;
  90–91 & 168–9, photographs by Peter Mautsch;
  192 & 197, photograph by Chris Chen)
Cover design by saso content & design pty ltd

Set in Leawood LT 10/15 pt; Futura LT Book 11/15pt;
Bell Gothic 11/15pt.

Printed and bound by Griffin Press, Adelaide

5 4 3 2 1

Contents

Who we are

SAVE: Your money, your time, your planet is our fourth book. The first, *Spotless*, was the biggest selling book in Australia in 2006 and is now available in Norway, Italy, UK and Brazil. *Speedcleaning* is also available in the UK and Italy, and the third book in the series is *How to be Comfy*. Each book looks at a different aspect of the home – how to clean it, organise it and create a haven. Now, find out how to reuse common household items in *SAVE*.

Shannon Lush is a wife and mother. She is also an artist and fine arts restorer who works in 27 mediums. She loves to collect handy hints and understand the chemistry behind them, and has never been stumped by a question regarding a stain on any of the numerous radio programmes she appears on, or for the magazine and newspaper articles she writes. She comes from a family that has a problem-solving attitude. On recent radio programmes she has been asking listeners the question 'What did you throw out last?' and has managed to find an alternative use for every item. Everything from banana peels to old couches can have a new life.

Jennifer Fleming is a writer, media consultant and ABC broadcaster. Her knowledge of cleaning and stain removal has expanded considerably since working on these books. She hails from a family that composts and always separates paper from plastic. While not quite at the stage of creating welcome mats from old bread bags, she now reuses old spice jars. Her work at ABC Radio in Sydney means she's informed about the latest research and thinking on many issues.

Acknowledgements

Many people have helped bring this book to life. Thanks to Shannon Lush for her expertise; to agent Elizabeth Troyeur for patiently looking after the fine print; and to Karen Penning, Brigitta Doyle, Jane Finemore and the team at ABC Books. Editor Megan Johnston made excellent and thoughtful suggestions. Thanks to Nanette Backhouse for her design and Alan Laver for his illustrations. Thanks also to family and friends: Pat and John Fleming (who read many drafts), Jason Maher, Virginia Lloyd, Brett Stone, Anthony Donohue, Tony Speede and James Valentine.

Jennifer

With every successive book we write, the list of people to thank gets longer and longer. So many people have helped so much: all of the wonderful radio producers and presenters I've worked with, including James Valentine, Richard Fidler, Annie Gaston, Kathie Bedford, Ingrid Just, Louise Saunders, Carol Whitelock, Genevieve Jacobs, Kirsten March and Glenn Barndon from the ABC; George and Paul from 2UE; and Graham Hill from Radio Live New Zealand. Thanks to all the wonderful people at ABC Books including my friend Jane Finemore, Karen Penning, Nanette Backhouse and too many others to list. A special thank you to all the wonderful people who send their questions to the magazines and newspapers I write for, or who call the radio stations for advice, and let me into a small part of their lives (even if it is the grubby part). Thanks to my partner in grime Jennifer Fleming, and my agent and friend Elizabeth Troyeur. But most of all to my wonderful, crazy, supportive family. A special thanks to my husband Rick and daughter Erin.

Shannon

Introduction

Do you have a drawer in your home filled with old gift-wrapping paper, bits of ribbon and other things you might be able to reuse? Do you have a shelf where old jars and plastic containers are kept? In days gone by everyone had areas in the home stocked with items to reuse: old coffee jars became containers for nails and screws; fraying business shirts were turned into quilts; and old shoe boxes became storage units. Reuse was very common. Today items are cheaper to buy and easy to throw away so we don't tend to hang on to them. We don't bother to reuse takeaway containers or old yoghurt tubs. When we get a new pair of sunglasses, we don't think to turn the old sturdy case into a box for jewellery. Without thinking too much about it, after we use something we throw it into the bin. It ends up in landfill and we end up having to buy something else to replace it. And here's the biggest sting: you're paying for it because all that packaging costs money! We want you to save money, save time and, in the process, help save the planet—all without losing your lifestyle.

This book takes you on a room-by-room tour through your home and suggests many alternative uses for common household items. It includes information on why it's important to change your habits, anecdotes of people making positive changes, and numerous money-, time- and planet-saving ideas. It encourages you to create a rag bag (where old clothes and fabric can be stored to use for cleaning or mending); start a busy box of odds and ends (such as broken ceramics, magazines and patchwork fabric for crafts); and begin a lumber pile (where old timber is stacked and stored for other uses). Some suggestions will take only a couple of minutes; others will require more time and ability. Some ideas will seem a bit over-the-top; others will seem obvious.

Today there's a new imperative to being less wasteful: the future of the planet. Our first-world lifestyle is comfortable and enjoyable but it's also choking us, literally—Australia has one of the highest asthma rates in the world. In some countries, people with heart and lung problems are finding it more difficult to breathe because of smog from cars and coal-fired power stations. There are threats to the Great Barrier Reef and the Murray-Darling river system. Even the Vatican is worried, nominating polluting as a new social sin!

Shannon and Jennifer remember how things were done in the more thrifty and resourceful not-so-distant past. As one of five children, Shannon recalls the family bin was never filled to the top. Instead, items were used up, paper bags were saved and rubber bands were never thrown away. There was less packaging, more composting and a spirit of 'make do and mend'. Going to the tip was an adventure as you searched for treasure among the trash. Now, she's horrified at what people throw away in the council clean-up.

While Jennifer is from Generation X, her parents are products of what she describes as 'Generation Frugal', the post-war generation when everything was scarce. One grandfather kept old leather boots in the shed to turn into tap washers. The other, a builder, had a slogan: 'Don't damage and don't waste'. Her dad uses old jars to store nails and screws. One of her mum's favourite mantras is 'Do you really need it?' which she thinks today's teenagers should be able to download onto their mobile phones before making yet another purchase.

During the writing of this book, Shannon decided to reuse all the recyclable material that came into her home. She turned old plastic bags into knitted coathanger covers, a crocheted hat and a hooked welcome mat, and found many uses for excess cardboard, tins and paper. Even though she has always been a careful recycler, the act of consciously finding new uses for old items really opened her eyes to just how much recyclable material goes into that yellow bin. If Shannon, with her incredibly busy schedule, can drop her recycling to nil for six weeks, surely we could all drop our recycling by 10 per cent without impacting on our lifestyle.

We hope *SAVE* will inspire you to hunt around in second-hand stores and give old or pre-loved furniture a new lease of life. The quality and character is often much better than that of brand new items and they are often much cheaper. If you can't find a use for something, donate it to charity or give it away to friends or family. We want you to reduce your electricity bill: the lower your bill, the lower your carbon emissions. Do you turn out the bedroom light when you're in the lounge room? Do you leave your appliances on stand-by when they are not in use? Are there any dripping taps in or around your house? By making small changes, you will save money and you'll be helping the planet at the same time.

We know some of you will be thinking: I don't have the space, what about all that clutter? And, yes, this can be a challenge if you hang on to everything without having an organisation system in place. Not all clutter is bad but it must be ordered so when you need a particular item you can put your hands on it straight away. Storage varies from home to home and some of you will be able to store more than others. Designate a drawer in the kitchen for odds and ends. Use a shelf in the linen press. Create hanging systems behind bedroom doors and in cupboards. Add hooks to the sides of cupboards, wardrobes or backs of doors. Construct shelves in laundries, sheds and garages. Use space under floors or inside the roof. Remember: you control the clutter, the clutter doesn't control you. If you don't have a lot of space, donate and recycle.

You might find your first days of downshifting a bit odd. And let's face it, it's hard to change long-standing habits and go against the consumerist grain. But over time, using old jars to make preserves, turning the last bit of toothpaste into a stain remover and making your own playdough for the children will feel normal and good and fun. Buck the trend and become part of a new community that saves, reuses and recycles.

We don't expect you to try all of the suggestions in this book. Our hope is that you'll be encouraged and inspired to think differently about items you throw away and about the volume of goods you consume.

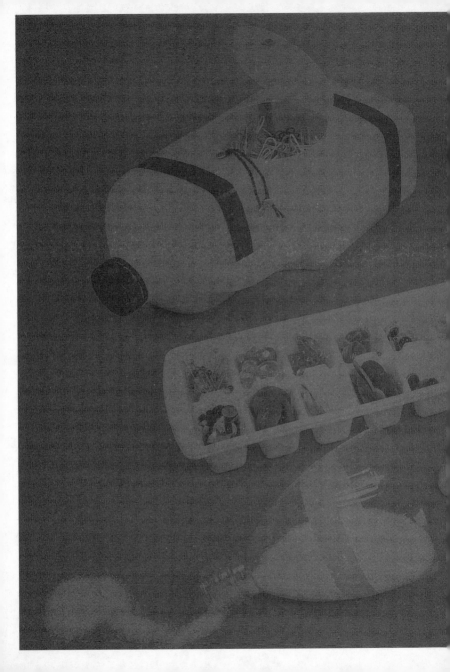

Kitchen

If you're like Shannon, the kitchen is the heart of your home. It's also a place for imaginative money-, time- and planet-saving ideas. When shopping, try to choose goods that are recyclable or have the least amount of packaging to save on landfill. We know it's difficult to avoid packaging altogether so we've included other ways to use it throughout your home. Where possible, choose paper and glass over plastics because they're more hygienic and easier to recycle. Glass is ideal because it can be reused safely over and over again.

> **SAVE FEATURE:** Fruits such as strawberries, blueberries and raspberries are generally packaged in plastic punnets. Rather than tossing the punnet away, wash it and turn it into a string holder. Just thread the string through one of the existing holes and store it somewhere that's easy to access. Your string stays clean and won't tangle.

Paper

When paper was scarce and costly, Shannon remembers using worn old paper bags or butcher's paper from the scrap-paper drawer to scribble down shopping lists. Paper packaging has come a long way since then. These days paper products come in all shapes and sizes and can be reinforced with wax or plastic, such as milk cartons. Other items have metal foil bonded to the paper, such as popper drinks, which means the paper is far more durable and reusable.

SAVE: *CARDBOARD CENTRE OF PAPER TOWEL ROLLS*
OTHER USES:

+ Use to **store rolled posters, paperwork or artwork**.
+ Use to **store pairs of socks, stockings and undies** in your drawers. Not only will it make them easy to stack and store, it also makes finding what you need simple because the fabric shows at the end.
+ Keep your **scarves and ties crease-free** by wrapping them around the roll.
+ Take excess rolls to a local **school or kindergarten** for craft projects.

TIP: Make your own Christmas bon bons. Buy the snaps (the things that make the popping noise when the bon bons are pulled) at a craft store and attach them with a piece of tape or glue to the inside of a thin cardboard roll. Place a paper hat, which you've made or recycled from last year, a joke of your own or one downloaded from the internet and a little gift inside. Wrap in colourful crepe paper, pages from a magazine or recycled gift paper, tie off the ends with string or ribbon and you're ready to pop!

DID YOU KNOW? *There's a group known as the Cardboard Tube Fighting League that reuses cardboard tubes for mock fighting. They might want your old tubes! Visit www.tubeduel.com.*

SAVE: CEREAL BOXES

OTHER USES:

+ Old cereal boxes can be converted into **document or magazine holders**. Cut one corner of the box at a 45-degree angle so it's big enough for your documents or magazines to fit inside. Decoupage or decorate the box with scrap fabric, leftover wallpaper, recycled gift-wrapping paper or spray paint. Before you decorate, spray the cardboard with a good-quality surface spray to deter bugs that love cardboard, such as cockroaches, beetles and moths.

+ If your shoes wear out quickly, add another layer of protection by making a **shoe liner**. Cut the cardboard to the shape of the inner sole and place it inside the shoe, grey side up. The cardboard helps spread the foot pressure and saves wear on the inner lining of your shoes. It also absorbs sweat and is easy to replace. Cardboard shoe liners help prevent the inner sole splitting in children's school shoes – a source of nasty blisters!

TIP: If you don't like the cardboard idea, make your shoes last longer by using felt as a shoe liner. Just cut the felt to size and place it inside your shoes.

SAVE: *BUTTER WRAPPING PAPER*

OTHER USES:

+ **Line cake tins** when baking. It's already greased and you'll save on baking paper. Don't use butter paper made or lined with foil.
+ **Grease cake tins and baking trays** by rubbing with butter or margarine paper. Store the paper folded in the freezer ready to use when you need it.

TIP: There's a concept known as 'pre-cycling' where you buy an item only if it can be recycled once you've finished using it. For instance, if a packet of biscuits has packaging that can't be recycled or reused, you make a decision not to buy them. Hopefully the manufacturer is motivated to change the way it packages goods.

SAVE: *PAPER BAGS*

OTHER USES:

+ Paper bags have **many handy uses**. They're a protective covering, reduce exposure to insects and also help items retain moisture (while still allowing air to flow). And they can be reused.

- **Dry and press flowers** (see pages 216–7).
- **Dry herbs, vegetables, fruit and rind** (see pages 39–40 and 85–7).
- **Store mushrooms**.
- **Speed up the ripening process of fruit.** Put the fruit in a paper bag with a banana. Bananas give off a chemical called ethylene that boosts the ripening process. You can turn a rock-hard avocado into a ripe one overnight!
- **Store** loose items, such as beads and buttons.
- Use for **art and craft projects**. Make an instant hand-puppet!

TIP: One of the easiest ways to save money is to make your lunch at home and take it to work in a recycled paper bag or lunchbox. The average sandwich costs $7.50 so if you take your lunch each day, that's a saving of $37.50 a week! A homemade sandwich costs around 80 cents to make.

SAVE: NEWSPAPERS

OTHER USES:

- Even though many people now read newspapers online, you're still likely to receive a local newspaper. Make use of it! In addition to wrapping up takeaway fish and chips, old newspaper is ideal for **lining the tops of cupboards** in the kitchen. It collects gunk and saves on cleaning.

+ Even though we don't advocate using fireplaces, if you do use one, **fire briquettes** made from old newspapers are great for starting a fire. Soak the newspaper in water (to remove bleach and toxins – the water is fine for the garden), squeeze out the water, shape the newspaper into balls and allow it to dry. Use only when completely dry.

+ Make **sewing patterns** for clothing or other items, such as slipcovers for the couch. You can even take the outline of your children's feet as a paper pattern and use it when shoe shopping if they're not with you, as Shannon's mum does.

+ Entertain the kids by making **papier-mâché**. Make sure there's some plastic covering (such as an old shower curtain) underneath your papier-mâché work area because it can get messy. Rip strips of newspaper 3 centimetres wide, place in a bucket of water and add 2 cups of wallpaper paste. To make the paste, combine 1 part plain flour with 2 parts water in a large saucepan and stir over a gentle heat until the mixture is thick and clear. For each cup of mixture, add 1 tablespoon of salt or 2 drops of oil of cloves to prevent mould. Scrunch the glue and paper together until it's like putty.

To make masks, blow up a balloon and layer the pulp over it, leaving two holes for the eyes, then put aside until it dries. Make a doll's body, limbs and head and sew them together while wet with a needle and tough thread or string. Make clothes for the dolly with fabric from your rag bag. Create toy furniture that's light and strong. You can even make your own fabulous Christmas decorations.

+ Newspaper is a great **deodoriser**. Shove it in shoes and leave overnight. Place a crumpled sheet of newspaper inside smelly plastic containers to remove nasty odours.

+ Shred newspapers to use as **mulch in the garden**. It will cut back on water use and reduce water evaporation.

+ Create a **no-dig garden** that's weed free. Put four layers of newspaper over the designated area and wet each layer with water. Cover the newspaper with a 10-centimetre thick layer of topsoil and fertiliser or potting mixture and mulch. The newspaper kills weeds and the elevated garden bed is easier to access if you have arthritis or difficulties with mobility.

+ **Wrap kitchen scraps** in newspaper and put into your bin. It's better for landfill and is what people used to do before plastic bags came along.

DID YOU KNOW? *According to Planet Ark,
Australians are the best recyclers of newspapers
and magazines in the world. In 2007, we recycled
the equivalent of 1 billion newspapers.*

SAVE: *FLOUR BAGS*
OTHER USES:

+ Flour bags use double-layered paper which is
  designed to keep moisture out. Use to **line tins**
  when disposing of excess fat.

SAVE: *OLD PAPER CUPS*
OTHER USES:

+ Shannon's Great-aunt Leticia used to carry a fold-
  up metal concertina cup in her handbag to drink
  cups of tea. These are still available from camping
  supply stores. Find out if your local café allows
  you to **use your own** cup or mug for takeaway
  rather than using a disposable paper cup.
+ Wash them clean with water (don't immerse the
  cup in water or it will disintegrate). Remove the
  base and use the container as a **funnel**.
+ **Protect seedlings** by removing the base of the cup
  and wedging it into the soil around the fledgling
  plant.
+ Put in the **kids' busy box**.

SAVE: MILK CARTONS

OTHER USES:

+ Waxed or plastic-coated cardboard cartons make great **freezer storage containers**. Just wash out with a little detergent and water before reuse. Pour soup, casseroles or stews into the cleaned cartons and place in the freezer. If you have a small freezer and can't rest the milk carton upright, place a plastic bag inside the milk carton, fill it up, tie off the bag tightly and secure the top of the carton with a peg or clip before lying it down. The cartons are easy to stack.

+ Cut off the top and **store excess cooking fat** in them. If you leave the fat on the benchtop, make sure it's covered or nasties will get in. If reusing the fat in cooking, it must be strained to remove any traces of cooked material. To sterilise the fat, cook over a medium-high heat to blue fume stage, which is just before it smokes and gives off a blue haze, and then strain. Never pour fat down the drain because it will clog and is bad for the environment. You can put fat in general household bins or find out if there's an oil recycler near you. Visit recyclingnearyou.com.au and look under 'oil-cooking'. The fat could be converted to biofuel.

+ Use as **candle moulds**. (For tips on how to make candles, see page 20, *How to be Comfy*.)

+ **Wash and squash** before recycling.

Can you put a pizza box in the paper recycling bin?

You'd think because the carton is made of cardboard it's fine to put in the recycling bin. But if it's covered in oil and food, it could contaminate other paper products. Some councils accept pizza boxes and others don't. It's best to check with your council (information is often on their website).

SAVE: *CARDBOARD ICE-CREAM CONTAINERS*

OTHER USES:

+ Use as a **gift box** for unusually shaped objects. Clean with a little dishwashing liquid and water but don't soak them or they'll disintegrate. Cover in leftover wallpaper, paint or wrapping paper.

+ Use as **seedling pots**. Once the seeds have germinated, bury the pot in the ground. The cardboard will disintegrate after about 6 months.

SAVE: *EGG CARTONS*

OTHER USES:

+ These have many other uses. They make instant **paint pots**.

+ Make into **toys**, such as alligators, monsters and trains.

+ Use to **store delicate Christmas decorations**, such as crystal or glass baubles.

+ **Decorate the carton** and present handmade chocolates in each casing.
+ Remove the top and place it in your office drawer as an **organiser** for clips, drawing pins, staples, paperclips, rubber bands etc.
+ Use to **sort and store jewellery** or any other small items.
+ Send to your local **school or kindy**.

 DID YOU KNOW? *Household recyclables are delivered to a Material Recovery Facility where they are sorted and baled into groups: paper, cardboard, plastics, glass, steel and aluminium. They are then sent for remanufacture.*

Plastic

Plastic water bottles have become the environmental equivalent of plastic bags: a new pariah. Some environmental groups are even directing people not to buy bottled water but drink tap water instead. Aside from the petrochemicals and the amount of energy it takes to make and transport bottled water, environmentalists also argue there are more regulations over tap water than bottled water. If it's taste you're worried about, a *Choice* magazine panel found people couldn't distinguish between two branded bottles of water and Sydney tap water. If your local water supply isn't to your taste, use a water filter. Another concern with bottled water is Australia doesn't have great away-from-home recycling facilities: for example, if you drink a bottle of water at the movies and throw the empty bottle in a bin, the plastic isn't recycled but goes into landfill. There's also a huge mark-up on the price of bottled water. One survey found bottled water served with meals is 500 times more expensive than tap water and 300 times more damaging to the environment.

SAVE: PLASTIC BOTTLES

OTHER USES:

+ The most obvious use for old plastic bottles is to **put tap water** in them and place them in the fridge so they're ready when you need them.
+ Turn them into a **terrarium**, or mini-greenhouse, for seedlings. Cut the bottle in half, put soil and seeds in the bottom part of the bottle and place the other part of the bottle on top.
+ Turn them into **shakers** for children. Add rice, dried pasta or lentils to the bottle and put the lid back on. It makes an instant musical instrument!

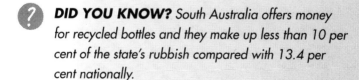

DID YOU KNOW? *South Australia offers money for recycled bottles and they make up less than 10 per cent of the state's rubbish compared with 13.4 per cent nationally.*

SAVE: *POLYSTYRENE NETTING*

OTHER USES:

+ Delicate fruits, such as mangoes or papayas, often come wrapped in netting. Scrunch up the netting and wipe it over the lint catcher in the dryer to **remove lint**.

+ Use for **art and craft projects**.

+ Use to provide **grip and insulation** on water bottles and cans of drink.

TIP: Unfortunately, biscuit wrapping doesn't recycle well because it's made of cellulose and plastic. Put it in your household garbage. Reuse the trays to store small items in your sewing kit or workshop. Shannon uses biscuit trays in her sewing box to store bobbins.

SAVE: *MILK BOTTLES*

OTHER USES:

+ The plastic used in milk bottles is easy to cut with scissors. Cut 2-litre bottles in half and use the top part as a **funnel**.

+ Using a 4-litre bottle, cut off the top of the lid at an angle to create a **watering can**. Use the handle as a spout.

+ Cut diagonally across the body of the bottle, discard the bottom part and you've got a **scoop**.

Use in the garden or the kitchen to scoop flour
or dried foods, such as beans, rice, nuts.

+ Cut a hole into the side of a 4-litre milk bottle so
  it's big enough for your hand to fit into. Use it to
  store small items such as paperclips or pins.

+ Use it to mix **pancake batter**. Combine 1 cup of
  plain flour, 1 cup of milk, ¼ teaspoon of salt and
  1 egg in the bottle, put on the lid and shake. The
  batter is ready to pour straight into the pan—and
  is much cheaper than the commercial ones!

+ Make a **mini-bucket** for the kids to use. Cut the spout
  and handle off, punch a hole in either side of the
  container and attach string. Use it to catch tadpoles.

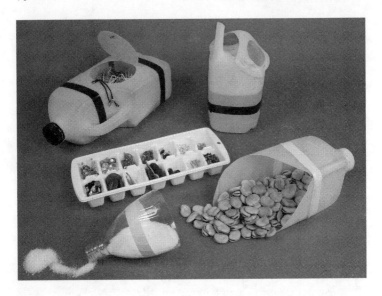

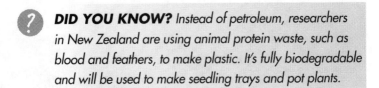

TIP: Keep chilled water in the fridge so you don't
waste water waiting for it to cool from the tap.

? DID YOU KNOW? *Instead of petroleum, researchers
in New Zealand are using animal protein waste, such as
blood and feathers, to make plastic. It's fully biodegradable
and will be used to make seedling trays and pot plants.*

SAVE: MARGARINE CONTAINERS

OTHER USES:

+ Wipe them out with paper towel and **store nuts
and bolts** in them. The residual oils prevent rust and
it's easy to write what's inside using a marker pen.

SAVE: *PLASTIC CUTLERY*

OTHER USES:

+ Take on **picnics**.
+ **Shrink** takeaway plastic cutlery. Hold the handle over a stove until it's soft and touch the soft end to a breadboard so it rolls up and can fit into a lunchbox.

TIP: Make shrinkies from chip packets or other plastic packaging. Set the oven at the lowest temperature, put the chip packet or packaging on baking paper and place inside the oven. Keep an eye on it and remove when it's the size you want it to be. If you want to be able to hang it, use a hole punch on one corner before putting the packet in the oven. That way, your kids can hang the shrunken items from their school bags! It's a great way to make toy grocery items for the toy box.

SAVE: *NETTING*

OTHER USES:

+ Use old fruit bag netting to **store pegs**. If you want to hang it from the clothesline, place a wire coathanger on a table, pull the hook sideways 90 degrees and turn the triangle part into a circle. Place the opened end of the fruit bag netting around the circle part of the coathanger and stitch or staple into position. It's ready to hang from your clothesline. When it rains, water can run through it and your pegs won't collect mould or debris.

+ **Wash loose vegetables** in netting. You can clear the dirt and pick up the vegies in one go.
+ Secure over a **drain hole** to stop clogging or to prevent bugs getting into your home. Cut the netting slightly larger than the hole, unscrew the grill across the drain, place the netting over the hole and screw the grill into place. The grill thread will keep the netting in place.

SAVE: ICE-CUBE TRAYS

OTHER USES:

+ Keep in a **sewing box** to sort bits, beads and buttons.
+ Keep in a **fishing box** to sort sinkers and other gear.
+ Make ice-cube trays (you can only use the ones

that bend) into **lanterns**. Turn the tray inside out to make a circle and staple the edges together. Only use tealight or votive candles so the tray doesn't melt. You can also wrap bendy ice-cube trays around fairy lights for a unique light effect.

SAVE: *TAKEAWAY CONTAINERS AND LIDS*
OTHER USES:

+ These are the ultimate storage solution for so many things, especially **leftover food**. Because plastic absorbs oils and smells, wash containers separately in dishwashing liquid and water.
+ Use as **lunchboxes**.
+ Use to **store chopped vegetables** in the fridge. Add a little lemon juice to the vegies to prevent browning. Encourage your children to snack on the pre-chopped vegies rather than eating rubbish.
+ They're great for mixing and storing **lotions and potions**.
+ Store **cleaning products** in them. Just add a label so you know what's inside and make sure you keep them out of children's reach!
+ Keep **tail ends of ribbons** and hair clips inside.
+ Use lids as a **divider in a box** for your files or recipe cards.

TIP: Don't use takeaway containers to store food if the plastic surface isn't slick and smooth because they're no longer hygienic. Transfer them to the potting shed, garage or laundry.

DID YOU KNOW? *When reheating food, some containers are preferable to others. Whenever you heat plastic-based containers in the microwave, you increase the chance of chemicals being released. Only use plastics that have been designed for cooking and opt for heat-resistant glass or ceramics instead. Microwave plastic wraps, baking paper, cooking bags, parchment paper and white microwave-safe paper towels are fine to use.*

TIP: Don't let plastic wrap touch foods during microwaving. Never use thin plastic storage bags, brown paper (unless microwave-safe), plastic grocery bags or newspaper when microwaving. Only use foil if it's immersed in water and wrapped entirely around something, such as a chicken leg. Otherwise, the foil will arc or short out your microwave.

TIP: Wipe the inside of the microwave after each use with pantyhose ball dipped in white vinegar so food doesn't harden and become more difficult to remove. You'll save time!

DID YOU KNOW? *2005 Nobel Peace Prize winner Wangari Maathai argued plastic bags can lead to the spread of malaria. If old bags become filled with rainwater this creates the perfect breeding ground for mosquitoes which carry the disease. As a result, Kenya has banned the production and distribution of light-density bags.*

SAVE: PLASTIC BAGS

→ There's been a lot of discussion about reducing the use of plastic bags. If you don't use green carry bags at the supermarket, **reuse your old plastic** ones. Some supermarkets have return bins to recycle them.

→ You've probably never thought to **wash** your plastic bags and hang them on the line to dry to reuse again and again. When Shannon was growing up, plastic bags were rare and were always seen hanging on clotheslines. She always brought bags home from school and reused them.

OTHER USES:

+ Use as **bin liners** for non-recyclable material.
+ **Weave, knit, crochet or plait plastic bags** into a range of waterproof items, such as baskets, handbags, mats and coat-hanger covers. Shred different coloured bags into long thin strips and use them to create different patterns. For pattern ideas, visit www.myrecycledbags.com. Shannon has a fishing hat made from used plastic bags.

Crocheted hat, knitted coathanger covers and hooked welcome mat all made from plastic bread bags and shopping bags.

+ Use plastic bags to **remove pollen** heads from lilies. Place the bag over your hand, remove the pollen and wrap the bag over the top. Place in the bin or use the pollen to make your own yellow dye.
+ Keep a plastic bag in your handbag. You may need to carry extra items or **wrap up something wet**.
+ Use to **pick up dog poo**.
+ Use to **line school bags** to avoid cleaning out squashed banana.
+ If you carry lots of things, **line your handbag** with a plastic bag so you avoid staining. This also increases the life of your handbag.
+ A large plastic bag can double as a **poncho** when it rains.
+ If you're painting and need a break, **wrap up the paintbrush** in a plastic bag so the paint doesn't dry out on the brush.

DID YOU KNOW? The Chinese government has banned the production and distribution of the thinnest plastic bags. This is expected to save 37 million barrels of oil. The bags are banned from all forms of public transport and scenic locations because hey get caught in trees and cause what's known as 'white pollution'.

CHANGE FOR GOOD: Two British Church of England ministers asked their congregations to reduce their carbon emissions for Lent as part of a 'Carbon Fast'. Parishioners were asked to avoid using plastic bags, give the dishwasher a day off, insulate the hot-water tank and check the house for draughts. Those taking part were asked to remove one light bulb from a prominent place in their home and live without it for 40 days.

TIP: The easiest way to store plastic bags is in a fabric sausage-shaped bag. Make or buy one. To make one, take a 30 x 30-centimetre square of fabric, fold it in half and sew a seam along one side. Hem either end and thread elastic through each hem. Add a handle or hook so it can be hung. Shove the plastic bags in one end and remove from the other.

 DID YOU KNOW? Most people know the damage plastic bags cause to marine life but did you know they were a major factor in severe flooding in Bangladesh because the bags clogged drains? The government imposed bans in 2002.

SAVE: STRAWS

OTHER USES:

+ Use to **extend make-up brush handles**. Place the straw over the handle.
+ **Rescue objects from a drain** by securing the top of the straw over the dropped item and retrieving it.
+ Put in the **kids' busy box**. They're easy to cut, stick or staple together!

SAVE: PLASTIC ICE-CREAM CONTAINERS

OTHER USES:

+ **Store nails or screws** for the workshop.
+ **Transport food** or other items to picnics and parties.
+ When Shannon was young, she used to **keep ribbons and hair bits** in old ice-cream containers. On ironing day, she'd get out the container and iron her ribbons for the week.

SAVE: POLYSTYRENE TRAYS

OTHER USES:

+ A lot of fruit and vegetables are packaged on trays. Clean the trays in dishwashing liquid and water and reuse to **package gifts**. Keep them stacked and ready for use.
+ Use as a **plant saucer or paint palette**.
+ Pierce holes in them and place at the bottom of

the **crisper drawer** in your fridge to allow air to flow around fruit and vegetables.

DID YOU KNOW? *Even though some polystyrene has a number 6 stamped on it, most councils don't accept it in recycling collections. But the EPS industry group coordinates recycling of polystyrene. To find out where the collection facility is in your state, visit www.repsa.org.au.*

SAVE: PUNNETS

OTHER USES:

+ Use as a holder for oasis sponge when **arranging flowers**. This stops it from crumbling.
+ **Wrap small items for sending in the post**. It's a great lightweight alternative to bubble wrap.
+ Turn them into a **string holder** (see page 2).

DID YOU KNOW? *The NSW Food Authority found up to 40 per cent of children could be at risk of food poisoning because they had warm lunchboxes. Lunchboxes without icepacks and sandwiches in paper bags were up to 12°C warmer than lunchboxes with frozen drinks or icepacks. There were five times the bacteria after 5 hours. To help keep lunchboxes cool, put ice-cubes in a plastic bag, tightly secure the top and place in the lunchbox.*

TIP: Zip-lock bags can be washed and used again. Dry on the clothesline and use until they form holes.

SAVE: *BINS*

OTHER USES:

+ Depending on the size, use as a **bucket**.
+ Store **toys** in them.
+ Use them to **store dry pet food** with or without its packaging. Scoop as you need it but keep the lid of the bin secured at other times.

SAVE: *JAR LIDS*

OTHER USES:

+ Use as a **desk organiser**. Place several lids in an office drawer and store items such as paper clips in them.
+ Use as a **pot plant saucer**.

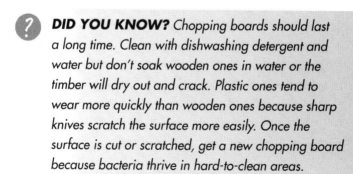

DID YOU KNOW? *Chopping boards should last a long time. Clean with dishwashing detergent and water but don't soak wooden ones in water or the timber will dry out and crack. Plastic ones tend to wear more quickly than wooden ones because sharp knives scratch the surface more easily. Once the surface is cut or scratched, get a new chopping board because bacteria thrive in hard-to-clean areas.*

Metal

Wander through a shed owned by someone born before the 1960s and you're bound to see an array of tin cans and glass jars housing nails, screws and other workshop items. Why buy new containers when you can recycle existing containers for free? The metal in tin cans makes a great craft material because it's malleable and easy to cut. Shannon is amazed that recycling slowed during the hippie era.

SAVE: *TIN CANS*

OTHER USES:

+ These are ideal to store **excess fat** before disposing in your household garbage.
+ Wrap a ribbon around a tin and **create a vase** for informal flower arrangements.
+ Use tall tin cans to make a base or legs for a **shelf** in the kitchen to stack spices. Use it as a bookshelf. Decorate the cans with fabric, paint or used gift-wrapping paper. Add extra stability by filling the cans with sand or soil.

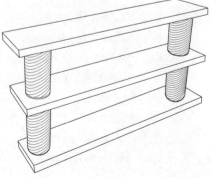

+ Spray paint or cover the cans in decorative paper or fabric from the rag bag and use as **pen holders**.
+ Make an old-style **tin-can telephone** for your kids. Take two tin cans, make a hole in the bottom of each tin and thread some string between the two. When the string is taut, voice vibrations pass along the string. Sadly, no texting is possible!
+ Label and use tins to hold solvent when **cleaning paintbrushes**.
+ Large cans can be turned on their sides to make a **wine rack**. Attach the cans using a hot glue gun.
+ Make outdoor **candle holders**. Punch holes in the side of the tins for the light to get through.
+ Use to make **filigree**! Remove the top and rim of a tin can with a can opener and cut fine strips down

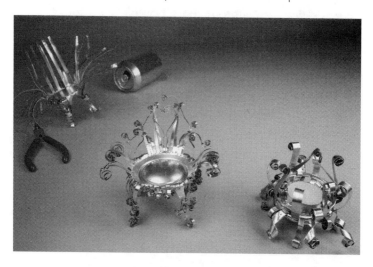

the side of the can using a pair of tin snips. Twist the strips into curls or whatever shape you want using pliers. You can also use aluminium cans for filigree. Make a tealight candle holder, dolls' furniture or decorator baskets.

TIP: When you've exhausted all the uses for tin cans, apply the 'wash and squash' principle. Wash the tin, flatten it and place it in the appropriate recycling bin. It will take up less space.

SAVE: *OLD TEA STRAINERS*
OTHER USES:
+ Use to strain children's **poster paints**.
+ Use when making **tinctures**.
+ Add to the **children's tea set** and toy box for numerous straining activities.

SAVE: *JAR LIDS*
OTHER USES:
+ Use to **protect the floor** by placing lids under heavy furniture. The lid provides a larger surface area. You could even spray paint them in the same colour as the furniture or cover in the same material as the couch so they blend in.

SAVE: *STEEL WOOL*

OTHER USES:

+ Use to **fill or stuff** holes. Steel wool is particularly good at keeping out mice and rats because they can't eat through it. Birds don't like it either.

TIP: Keep your steel wool rust free by storing it in the freezer in a zip-lock bag.

SAVE: *CUTLERY*

OTHER USES:

+ Old cutlery is great to use in the **garden**. Use spoons to create seedling holes. Forks can be used to remove weeds from the lawn.
+ Use old knives in the shed to **spread glue or trim things**.
+ **To soften the edge** of tin cans or glass, run a serrated knife over the edge like a file.
+ To make a **fine chisel**, cut the blade of a knife 2 centimetres from the handle.
+ Make your own rustic **wind chimes**: flatten out the cutlery, make a hole in each handle, thread wire through each hole and suspend in the breeze.
+ Use to make **jewellery and belt buckles**. Twist fork tines into any design you like and turn into lovely bracelets.
+ Use knives as weeders **in the garden**. They will

rust (eventually) but are great to cut roots. Trim the roots around a pot when re-potting.

+ Cut a butter knife across the blade 5 centimetres from the handle and sharpen the leading edge. Use as a scraper for cleaning glass or as a **leadlighting tool** to cut leads and calmes.

+ Old knives can be turned into **paint scrapers** to access fiddly areas.

+ Use knives in **bonsai** work.

TIP: If your cutlery has rust marks from being cleaned in the dishwasher, don't throw it out! Scrub with a paste of bicarb and water.

SAVE: UTENSILS

OTHER USES:

+ **Slotted spoons** are ideal for mixing paint.

+ Use **egg flips** to scrape up spills on the floor. They make instant shovels for children in the garden or sandpit.

+ **Egg beaters** can help mix paint or fertiliser.

+ Place **stainless steel skewers** in tree trunks to hang plants from. They won't rust or harm the tree.

SAVE: POTS AND PANS

OTHER USES:

+ **Mix paint** in them.

+ Mix soil and sand for **potting** in them.

+ Turn into **pots for plants**.
+ Use as **storage** in the garage.
+ Turn them into **toys** for the kids' sandpit.
+ Take aluminium ones to the **recycler** and get money for them.

TIP: To clean stainless steel, wipe over with a pair of pantyhose dampened with white vinegar and dry with another pair of clean pantyhose.

SAVE: BAKING TINS
OTHER USES:

+ Use as a **desk organiser** or dressing table organiser. Decorate it with paint and one of grandma's doilies.
+ Use to **soak engine parts** in oil in the garage.

Glass

Hang on to glass jars because they can be reused in so many different ways. They're particularly handy for storing items you need to be able to see. And glass is easy to sterilise, so it's ideal for storing food.

SAVE: OLD DRINKING GLASSES
OTHER USES:

+ If chipped, smooth the edges around the chip with a sapphire nail file so you don't cut yourself. Use as a **tealight-candle holder**. If feeling creative,

etch a design into the glass with frosting cream
(see page 146 in *How to be Comfy*).

+ If big enough, use in the bathroom to **hold
toothbrushes and toothpaste**.

SAVE: GLASS JARS

OTHER USES:

+ Sterilise by immersing in boiling water for 2 minutes
and allow to air-dry or place on a tray in a cold
oven and heat to 110°C. When the oven reaches
temperature, turn it off and leave until the bottles
are cool enough to pick up. Remove the labels as
described below. Use to store **homemade jams,
pickles and preserves**. Keep in the pantry for
presents.

+ They make great **canisters**. To make different
sized jars match, decorate the lids in the same
colour. Lay fabric over the top, glue on and trim
the excess. Use the canisters to store whatever you
like. Remember to place a label on the jar or store
the label inside the jar.

+ Use to **store pins, buttons, nails or screws**.

How to remove a sticky label from a jar
Have you noticed sticky labels are even stickier? There
are several ways to remove them depending on what the
glue is. For loosely glued ones, fill the glass jar with hot

water but don't get the label wet. Put the lid on and leave for 10 minutes. The label will peel off. If any label remains, put a drop of dishwashing liquid and a little water on some plastic wrap, mix together and place the plastic wrap over the label. Leave for 10 minutes. The label should come off when you remove the plastic wrap. For stickier labels, apply tea tree oil with a cotton ball. Stronger still is eucalyptus oil applied with a cotton ball. If none of these techniques work, it's time to apply some heat. Aim a hair dryer at the label to melt the glue.

TIP: Transfer cooking oil from plastic bottles to glass ones and store in a cool place away from light. Oil lasts longer in glass and away from light.

DID YOU KNOW? *Glass recyclers use optical sorting technology to remove Pyrex dishes, crockery and drinking glasses from glass recycling bins. These melt at a different temperature to other glass and need to be recycled seperately.*

SAVE: BEER AND WINE BOTTLES

OTHER USES:

+ These bottles are incredibly strong. Use them to create a **garden edge** by wedging the top of the bottle into the ground until the base is 5 centimetres above the ground.

+ Use as **vases or candle holders**.
+ Turn into a **rolling pin**. To increase the weight of your rolling pin, fill with water and cork tightly.

How to cut glass

You'll need a glass cutter, which can be bought cheaply at the hardware store. Mark your edge by putting sticky tape where you want to cut the glass. Then run the cutting wheel, which will make a screeching noise, next to it. Rotate the cut end of the bottle over a flame and rub with ice until the glass separates and pops off. Carefully smooth the cut edge with a sapphire nail file. You can turn wine bottles into great vases.

The San Pellegrino factor

These lovely bottles are ideal for reuse because they've only contained water and are easy to clean. Use them to store your own herb- and spice-infused oils. Place good-quality olive oil in a bottle, add the herbs and allow to infuse for about 3 months. You can flavour vinegar in the same way. Keep or give as presents.

TIP: If you're feeling creative, decorate old bottles with *Cerne Relief* paint, which creates a cloisonné effect. The paint is available at craft and paint stores.

SAVE: MICROWAVE PLATE

OTHER USES:

+ Use as a **serving platter**. It's perfect for a cheese platter.
+ Because it's footed, you can place it on top of bowls in the fridge to create a **new shelf**.

SAVE: CHINA

→ China and ceramics can last for thousands of years. If you care for yours properly, it could last just as long (even though you won't be around to enjoy it!).

OTHER USES:

+ Once plates become chipped or crazed, it's best not to use them for food because bacteria can thrive in the cracks. Instead, use the plates as **pot plant saucers**.
+ Because paint doesn't dry out as quickly on porcelain, they make great **paint palettes**.
+ For china that's broken beyond repair, use in **mosaics** (see page 92). Keep broken china in a busy box.
+ To allow **drainage** in pot plants, place broken bits of china at the bottom of the pot. It's an ideal alternative to gravel.
+ Turn a damaged coffee mug into a **toothbrush holder** in the bathroom.

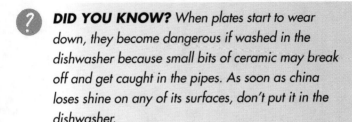

DID YOU KNOW? *When plates start to wear down, they become dangerous if washed in the dishwasher because small bits of ceramic may break off and get caught in the pipes. As soon as china loses shine on any of its surfaces, don't put it in the dishwasher.*

DID YOU KNOW? *An average dishwasher uses 40 litres of water; washing dishes in the sink uses 15 litres of water.*

SAVE: *SALAD BOWLS*

OTHER USES:

+ Use for a **cactus garden**.
+ Use as a **storage** container for items such as swimming goggles.
+ Use to **transport items**, such as vegetables from the vegie patch.

SAVE: *HERB AND SPICE JARS*

OTHER USES:

+ You can remove and replace the plastic shaker on the top of the jar with a knife. Then **refill** jars with spices or herbs bought at the shops or dried at home. Once refilled, return the plastic shaker to the top of the jar.
+ After cleaning with dishwashing liquid and water,

refill with hundreds and thousands, desiccated coconut or icing sugar. Or use it to dispense glitter! Buy big, inexpensive plastic bags of glitter at the hardware store and transfer it.

+ Use to store **bicarb** for cleaning.

+ Use to **store salad dressing** when taking salads to work or school. That way the lettuce won't become soggy.

+ Sterilise by immersing in boiling water for 2 minutes and allow to air dry or place on a tray in a cold oven and heat to 110°C. When the oven reaches temperature, turn it off and leave until the bottles are cool enough to pick up. Use to **store baby food**. They're narrow and tall making them less likely to break and small spoons fit inside them. Label them and keep a stack ready to go.

How to dry herbs

To dry leafy herbs, such as sage, basil and mint, chop the leaves into 3-millimetre thin strips making sure to cut across the leaf, not down it. Cutting across the leaf releases more volatile oils and more flavour. Put the cut herbs in a brown paper bag and store in a cool, dark place. Over the course of a week, shake the bag every morning and evening to loosen the leaves so moisture doesn't build up. To dry twiggy herbs, such as lavender, rosemary and cinnamon, tie them in a bundle and hang them in a dark corner until dry. Hanging them upside down means all the nutrients go to the head of the herb for greater flavour. The length of time they take to dry depends on the weather.

TIP: Don't throw out old herbs and spices that are past their use-by date. They can be used in potpourri, added to bicarb to remove odours or heated in the microwave and placed under dinner plates. Add a spicy aroma to a gift by rubbing herbs in some tissue paper and wrapping it around the gift.

How to make your own herbal tincture

Many herbal products are expensive and you can make your own. Just add 1 tablespoon of dried herbs and 2 tablespoons of denatured alcohol (available from the chemist) to a glass jar and cover. Leave the solution in the dark at room temperature for 4 days. Shake the jar every day. Strain the solution through a tea strainer or some muslin cloth into another jar. Label your creation. Use the appropriate tincture in perfumes, lotions, cleaning formulas or pesticides.

Paraphernalia

SAVE: STRING

OTHER USES:

+ Use to **wrap parcels and presents**.
+ **Tie up plants** in the garden or bundle up green waste.
+ **Repair handles on frying pans** (see page 87 of *How to be Comfy* for details).
+ Use for many **kids' projects**, including making mobiles and contraptions.
+ Use for **flower arranging**. Winding string along the stems of posies gives them a rustic look.
+ Create a **nautical look** by winding string around the outside of a tin can so it's completely covered. Attach the string to the tin with glue.

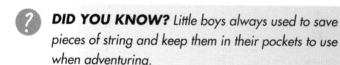

DID YOU KNOW? *Little boys always used to save pieces of string and keep them in their pockets to use when adventuring.*

SAVE: OLD CORKS

→ The advent of screw-top wine bottles means there are fewer corks around but if you get one, don't throw it away.

OTHER USES:

+ Corks can be cut into discs and placed on the back **corners of paintings** to protect the wall and allow air to circulate behind your art.

+ Use a cork as a **stopper for a soft drink bottle** if a lid goes astray.

+ Cork is perfect for **holding pins and needles**. It keeps them dry and rust free.

+ Use as a **doorstop**. Cut a cork in half lengthways, secure it between the door and the frame and the door will stay ajar.

+ **Protect skirting boards** from door marks by placing some cork where the door hits.

+ To **stop doors from rattling**, cut a cork into slithers and place along the doorjamb.

+ Make a **base for soap** by cutting champagne corks in half lengthways and placing half on either end of a cake of soap. Use hot water to wet the cork so it sticks to the soap. Your soap won't become gluggy sitting in water and there'll be less soap scum to clean up.

+ Cut cork into discs and fix with PVA glue to the bottom of **chair legs**. This reduces noise and protects the flooring.

+ Use cork to make **stamps**. Cut shapes into the bottom of the cork with a knife or burn patterns by heating a knife and cutting into the cork.

+ Make your **breadboard non-slip** by cutting wine corks into 1-centimetre thick discs and gluing them to the underside of the board.

+ Make a **noticeboard**. You may have some cardboard or ply timber around the house or you can buy some fairly cheaply. Cut it to size and glue slices of cork over the entire surface with PVA glue. Place two screw-in eye hooks at each top corner, thread fishing wire or string through the hooks and hang the board from a wall.

SAVE: *RUBBER GLOVES*
OTHER USES:
+ The fingers tend to disintegrate first but the material in the wrist area can be cut into large **rubber bands**. Shannon uses them to hold her make-up case together. They're ideal for securing kids' lunchboxes or manila folders, diaries and notebooks. Use the rubber bands to sort pens and pencils in children's pencil cases.
+ **Cut off the fingers and use them over broom handles** to make them non-slip, as a finger card for turning pages or to cover one finger when spreading glue.
+ Use bands cut from fingers over **saucepan handles** for grip.
+ Glue strips of rubber **under bathmats** to make them non-slip.

SAVE: *TEA TOWELS*
OTHER USES:
+ Use tea towels until they're completely threadbare! Linen has a strong weave and is great as **patching fabric**.

DID YOU KNOW? *Most modern tea towels are made of cotton because it's cheaper than linen but linen tea towels are far superior because they don't leave lint behind. They last for longer and absorb more water.*

SAVE: SPONGES

OTHER USES:

+ These can be easily cut with scissors and have a **range of other uses**. Before reusing them, wash in the washing machine and dry in the sun so you don't transfer dirt and bacteria. Alternatively, soak a dirty sponge in white vinegar for half an hour, wring it out and leave in the sunshine to dry.

+ Use old sponges to **clean venetian blinds**. Cut a sponge in half and place on the inner edges of a pair of tongs. Secure the sponges with a rubber band (or bands refashioned from rubber gloves). To clean the blinds, pinch and pull the tongs along each slat. To give an extra clean, add some white vinegar to the sponge. If you don't finish cleaning the blinds, leave a peg on the slat so you know where you're up to.

+ Place under the **legs and edges of furniture** to protect floors. Cut them to size and glue them on with hot glue.

+ Put them **behind paintings and mirrors** to allow

air-flow and prevent bugs and dust from gathering. Attach with Blu-Tack.

+ Stop your washing machine walking across the floor and **reduce the noise** by placing sponges under the feet. This is particularly useful for people who live in apartments.

+ Soak in children's paint and place in a takeaway container to use as a stamp pad for potato prints.

How to make your own dishwashing liquid

Get a shaker box (mesh box) and put the tail ends of soap inside. When it's time to do the washing up, put in the plug and shake the mesh box under hot water to generate frothy soap. Another option is to put shaved soap and water in a container, cover and shake vigorously. You can also do the washing up using just hot water, bicarb and white vinegar.

TIP: After washing up, pour a jug of hot water over the dishes to remove any traces of dishwashing liquid.

SAVE: BASKETS
OTHER USES:

+ These make great **storage bins** for items such as swimming goggles.

+ Store **pegs** for the clothesline.

+ Turn into hanging pots. Line the basket with

newspaper or sphagnum moss. Poke chains or piano wire through the side of the basket and twist. Use a key ring or a curtain ring to hold the chain or piano wire together. Use at least three chains for stability.

+ **If taking a meal to a friend's house, transport** it in a basket that you're happy to leave behind. They can use it for the same purpose.

SAVE: PLASTIC PACKING TAPE

OTHER USES:

+ Weave into **baskets or shopping bags**.
+ If you lock your keys in the car, you can use it to **unlock your door**.

TIP: Cane and wicker baskets are washable. To clean very dirty ones, combine 1 kilogram of salt with 9 litres of water in a bucket and mix well. For mildly dirty ones, mix 1 cup of salt with 9 litres of water. Wash and leave in the sunshine to dry.

Fridges

→ When buying a fridge, look at the **energy rating**: the more stars the better. Select the most **appropriate size** for your needs.

→ Place the fridge in a **cool spot** away from the oven or direct sunlight.

→ A fridge with the **freezer compartment at the bottom is more efficient** than one with the freezer at the top.

→ Set the fridge at the **correct temperature** of 4°C. A change of 1°C can affect energy consumption by up to 5 per cent.

→ Leave a 5-centimetre gap between the back of the fridge and the wall to **allow ventilation**.

→ If unsealed, regularly **dust the coils** at the back of the fridge.

→ **Check the seals**. The seals around the fridge door should be able to hold a piece of paper when closed. If not, replace them.

→ Place older fridges on a **perforated board** to allow air to circulate underneath. The legs on older fridges aren't as high as newer ones.

OTHER USE:

+ Turn an old fridge into a **tool cupboard**. Because they're sealed, tools won't get rusty. Make sure it's got a child-safe latch so kids don't get locked in. Avoid musty smells by cleaning inside and out, including the seals, with white vinegar.

TIP: Keep the fridge almost full because it creates a thermal mass and will run more efficiently. The fuller the fridge, the better it runs. One idea is to freeze cooler bricks and place them in the fridge to keep the temperature cooler.

What to do with old appliances such as fridges

When people buy a new fridge, they often put the old one in the garage and turn it into a beer fridge (one-third of Australian households have two or more fridges). But this could spell unhealthy carbon emissions if the seals are loose or it's very old. It also adds to your energy bill to the tune of around $120 a year. To dispose of an old fridge, contact your council or visit www.recyclingnearyou.com.au. If keeping a second fridge, switch it off when not in use.

Dishwashers

→ Have a range of program settings to enable **water saving options**, including an economy cycle.

→ Have a dual **hot and cold water connection**. That way you can regulate the temperature and use less power. It's much cheaper to generate heat from your hot-water system than it is to use the element in your dishwasher.

→ Use the **economy cycle** for lightly soiled dishes.

→ **Clean the filter** regularly.

→ **Open the door after the final rinse cycle** to air-dry the dishes.

→ **Take advantage of cheaper off-peak water rates** by running the dishwasher overnight.

→ Use **environmentally friendly dishwashing**

detergents or bicarb (for detergent) and white vinegar (as a rinse aid).

OTHER USE:

+ Shannon hates dishwashers and uses hers to **store potatoes** and root vegetables.

Ovens

→ In Australia, sales of electric ovens outnumber gas ovens ten to one even though **gas ovens are cheaper to run**.

→ Whether electric or gas, **a fan-forced oven is more energy efficient** because heat is circulated more evenly making cooking quicker.

→ When using the oven, **cook several things at once and freeze excess food**.

→ To save energy, **use residual heat** by turning the oven off before you need to. The amount of radiant heat varies from oven to oven. Shannon turns her oven off 10 minutes before the meal is fully cooked.

→ When **igniting a gas stovetop**, don't turn it to the maximum level because it wastes the gas in the first puff of flame.

Microwaves

→ **Most people only use the microwave to reheat or defrost food**. If this is the case with you, an 800-watt microwave will do the job. Shannon has a 1200-watt microwave because she uses it a lot.

→ **The more functions a microwave has, the more efficient it is** because you can be very specific when using it.

→ To save money, **partially cook food in the microwave** and then brown it in the oven.

→ Always **cover food when cooking in the microwave** because it speeds up cooking time and helps retain vitamins.

→ **Turn the microwave off at the power point when you're not using it.** The display clocks use more energy than the microwave itself!

TIP: If buying more than one whitegood, ask for a discount for 'bundling'. Do research online and ask a store to match the lowest price you can find.

CHANGE FOR GOOD: In the 1990s, Australia banned the use of chlorofluorocarbons (CFCs) because they depleted the ozone layer, an important block for the sun's ultraviolet rays. The thinning ozone layer has led to more Australians being affected by skin cancer, cataracts and damage to the immune system.

TIP: Take old appliance boxes to your local school or kindy. They make great cubbies!

Food

How often have you piled your shopping trolley high with food, taken it home, put it in the fridge and about a week later, chucked a lot of it straight in the bin because it's gone off? You're not alone. A 2005 study by the Australia Institute found we spent $5.3 billion a year on food we didn't eat – estimated to be one supermarket bag worth of food for every three bags bought. This hurts your hip pocket and the planet. Smart shopping and cooking means less waste: so before you head to the shops, think about the meals you'll be preparing and write a list.

When you're shopping, check the ingredients list on packaged food. The fewer the number of ingredients, preservatives, colourings and flavourings, the better it's likely to be. Also consider how processed the food is and how many 'food miles' it's travelled before you buy it. Michael Pollan, author of *In Defense of Food*, recommends you don't eat food your great-grandmother wouldn't recognise! Fresh produce from growers' markets, farmers' markets or your local fruit and veg shop is likely to be fresher and last longer than that from supermarkets. Buy in season when food is plentiful and cheap and preserve it for later use.

> **SAVE FEATURE:** Don't throw away onion skins because they can be used to stain timber. Boil the skins in water for 15 minutes, strain and apply the liquid with a rag over timber. The mixture has the added benefit of deterring some insects. It also creates a deep rust, red-brown dye for wool.

Smart shopping strategies

How you shop will depend on the number of people in your household. But generally, it's a good idea to do a big shop once or twice a month and little shops in between. If you can, walk to your local shops for smaller purchases. Fewer trips to the supermarket will save time, petrol and your sanity!

The next time you're at the supermarket, notice what you smell as you enter. Many will have the smell of fresh bread. Why? Because the smell of bread makes you hungry and when you're hungry, you tend to buy more. Supermarkets use other tricks to make you part with more of your money, such as placing chocolate bars near the checkout where they're easy to reach (especially by little fingers), putting the most expensive items at eye level and locating essential items at opposite ends of the supermarket to make you walk down as many aisles as possible.

Be aware of the supermarket sales cycle and find out which day your supermarket re-stocks its shelves. The day before re-stock is generally bargain day. One research paper revealed shopping on Fridays can save up to 20 per cent on your grocery bill, particularly with fresh produce and meat. Catalogue specials tend to start on Mondays which is the best day for specials on long-life items such as toilet paper, bulk laundry powder, nappies and coffee. But be careful with perishables because it's likely bargain items are nearer to their use-by date. It's not a saving if the item is about to go off and you won't have the opportunity to use it.

Stock up when the Temporary Price Reductions (TPRs) are on. Obviously, you can't do this with perishable items unless they can be frozen, such as bread. Another option is to buy in bulk and share with neighbours or friends. Also watch for the items stacked at the end of aisles, known as 'gondola' fixtures. Companies pay to have their products placed here (and advertised in catalogues) to act as a volume driver to increase sales. There are bargains here but the trick is to work out the unit price. Is a discounted six-pack of toilet paper cheaper than a full price 10-pack? The way to work it out is to do the maths and see what one toilet roll in either configuration costs. For example, if a 10-pack costs $8.99, one roll is 89 cents. If a six-pack costs $5.99, one roll is 99 cents. In this scenario, the 10-pack is cheaper. Keep this in mind when buying in bulk. You can generally save money buying this way but not all the time. That's why it's a good idea to get into the habit of unit pricing. In one survey, the cost per gram of Vegemite in a 150-gram jar was half that of a 60-gram jar. An individual tea bag in a box of 25 was twice as expensive as in a box of 200. Some supermarkets include the unit price on the ticketing strip and there have been calls for all supermarkets to include this information so consumers can make informed choices.

TIP: Teach your children how to do unit pricing, to check use-by dates, ingredient lists and to weigh items. It helps them to learn about food, additives, measures and cost.

Another trick to watch for is the 'loss leader'. This is when an item is discounted to get you into the store in the hope you'll be dazzled by other items in the shop. A classic example is champagne at liquor stores. The price for a bottle is reduced from $85 to $59.95 and kept at the very back of the store. They want you to grab a couple of bottles of full-priced wine on your way to the checkout.

If you're aware of the tricks, you'll be less likely to fall for them.

TIP: If you can't find an item that's been advertised in a supermarket sales catalogue, ask! Some retailers may give you a raincheck.

Do you know what you're eating?

Many of us buy pre-prepared foods that are easy to heat and eat. But you might be surprised at what's actually in these foods. The best way to find out is to look at the ingredient panel which lists in order from most used ingredient to least used. Shannon checked out what was in a frozen apple pie and found preservatives, flavourings and colourings as well as artificial sweeteners and thickening agents, such as seaweed and gelatine. Gelatine comes from many sources including boiled animal bones and hides or agar. She thinks the apple pie should be renamed 'seaweed jelly'. If you make an apple pie yourself, it contains sugar, butter, flour, apples and water which is quite a different ingredient list. It goes to show you can't judge a pie by its packaging!

> *CHANGE FOR GOOD:* Rather than driving to the shops, walk and use a shopping trolley. They now come in plenty of funky designs, are easy to use and you'll get some exercise as well. According to www.climatefriendly.com, $50 a week on petrol equals 5.4 tonnes of greenhouse emissions per year that would cost $137.04 a year to offset.

Seasonal shopping

Fruit and veg are cheaper and tastier when in season. The easiest way to work out if something is in season is to watch the price: items are cheaper when they're in season. This ties in with 'food miles' or how far the food has travelled to get to you. It's better for the planet to buy food grown closest to you. Many fruit and veg stores have labels to show where food comes from. If they don't, ask!

Cheap meats

Just because you can't afford an expensive cut of meat doesn't mean you have to compromise on taste! It's all about how you prepare and cook it. In some households lamb shanks used to be thought of as bones for the dog but now, if cooked slowly with the right ingredients, they can be a signature winter dish.

Cheaper cuts of meat include chuck steak, veal shanks, lamb shanks and oyster blade. If the meat contains a bone, roast it slowly so the flavour from the bone and marrow infuses into the meat. Try this with lamb shanks, veal shanks and lamb necks (ask the butcher to remove the scent gland from the base of the neck). Chuck steak and oyster blade contain a lot of tendon material and muscle so they are great in slow-cooked meals such as casseroles, curries and stews. Bacon bits or off-cuts have less fat, are cheaper than rashers and add flavour to dishes such as quiches, soups and homemade pizzas. You'll also save money making a homemade pizza and it's quicker than ordering one in.

Marinating and tenderising meat is a great way to increase flavour. Some old-fashioned tricks include:

1. Crush papaya pips with a rolling pin and add to a marinade. If you leave the meat in this marinade for a couple of hours, you'll get a peppery taste in the meat. One papaya is enough for 2 kilograms of meat. Papaya contains the enzyme papain, which breaks down protein.

2. For each kilogram of meat, mix 1 teaspoon of bicarb, 1 teaspoon of olive oil and 2 tablespoons of wine or vinegar in a plastic bag or bowl. Add meat, try to remove all the air from the container and set aside for 2–3 hours.

3. For 1 kilogram of meat, crush 2 kiwifruit and combine with the meat in a plastic bag. The old sitting rule was 'half an hour for ½ an inch' (about 1 centimetre thickness

in modern measurements). Remove as much
air as possible from the bag. Kiwifruit contains the
protein-dissolving enzyme actinidin.

4. Wipe each side of the meat with a small amount of
avocado (which contains ethylene) and set aside for
half an hour per 1 centimetre in thickness. Remove the
avocado before cooking.

Chicken or beef?

We know it's challenging enough to decide what to eat at a
restaurant: there are taste and health considerations, but what
about environmental ones? A CSIRO and University of Sydney
report estimates that for every dollar spent (farm-gate prices)
beef generates 26.7 kilograms of greenhouse gases compared
with 3.2 kilograms for pigs and 2.4 kilograms for chickens.
They didn't include figures for lamb, kangaroo or fish.

SAVE: APPLE PEEL
OTHER USES:
+ Apple peel **cleans aluminium**. If a pot has egg or
cabbage stains, fill it with water, add apple peel
and bring to the boil. The stains will come away
from the pot.
+ To give **iron a rusty look** quickly, rub with some
apple peel or spray apple juice over it.
+ Apple gives off a lovely scent, especially in winter.

Put apple peel in a paper bag and leave in a
dark spot for a week, shaking each day. When
dried, **add to potpourri** and enjoy the fresh
fragrance.

TIP: Remove the smell of cabbage when cooking by
adding a slice of apple to the pot.

TIP: Save money by buying apples in season. You can
store them in the fridge for months at a time. The
way to tell if the apple is still edible is to tap on
the side with your knuckle. It should sound solid.

SAVE: AVOCADO

OTHER USES:

+ Once all the flesh is removed, run a cotton ball
  around the inside of the shell and use it as a **face
  mask** to clean and moisturise, minimise wrinkles
  and plump up crow's-feet. Also use as a moisturiser
  on your elbows, hands, heels and knees.
+ Use the skin as a **bowl for dip** at a party.
+ Use avocado as a **hair conditioner**. Massage
  1 tablespoon of avocado into your scalp, wrap
  your head in plastic wrap and leave for 20 minutes.
  Rinse out with warm water. The enzymes in
  avocado nourish the hair.

TIP: To store a cut avocado, run it under cold water and cover with plastic wrap before placing it in the fridge. Avocado can't be stored for long because it oxidises quickly.

SAVE: BANANAS

OTHER USES:

+ Speed up the **ripening process** of fruit by placing it in a paper bag with a banana. Banana gives off the ripening chemical ethylene.

+ Add banana skin to **compost** to speed up production. Chop the banana skin before adding it to the compost and then spray the compost with water. This allows the enzymes to travel throughout the compost.

+ Put whole skins into the water reservoir of tree ferns, birds'-nest ferns, elkhorns and other rainforest plants to **feed** them.

+ If a banana is overripe, store in the **freezer** until needed and use it to make smoothies, banana cake, banana bread, muffins and banana fritters.

> **CHANGE FOR GOOD:** To help children learn about food, Australian chef Stephanie Alexander set up the Kitchen Garden Foundation. Primary school children plant a vegetable patch, tend to it and then cook using the fresh ingredients from their garden. For more information, go to www.kitchengardenfoundation.org.au.

SAVE: BEER

OTHER USES:

+ Beer can be used to **wash your hair** and is a great fertiliser for mosses, lichens and ferns.
+ Non-alcoholic beer or hop tea **increases milk production** in breast-feeding mothers.
+ **Trap slugs** by placing beer inside half an orange peel. The slugs are attracted by the beer.
+ Use beer as a **meat tenderiser**. Pour it directly over steak while it's cooking on the barbecue. It also caramelises onions.

SAVE: BEETROOT (FRESH)

OTHER USES:

+ Many people throw beetroot leaves away but the small leaves are great in **salads** and the larger leaves can be steamed and served with finely chopped garlic and a squeeze of lemon juice.

You can also use the chopped leaves in **stir-fries** or any dish requiring spinach or silverbeet.

+ Beetroot makes a great **dye**. To create the dye, mix 1 cup of grated beetroot, 1 cup of salt and 2 litres of water in a saucepan. Bring to the boil for 2 minutes, strain and leave overnight. Use this liquid as a dye. Blueberries can be turned into a dye in the same way.

 DID YOU KNOW? *Shortages during WWII meant beetroot, onion skins, spinach and geranium leaves were used to dye clothes.*

SAVE: BOK CHOY AND CABBAGE

OTHER USES:

+ Use the leaves to reduce skin irritation and **relieve the pain of inflammation**.
+ Keep bok choy and cabbage leaves in the fridge and place a leaf inside your bra to **relieve mastitis**. This works by bringing blood to the surface of the skin.
+ Use as a **poultice** to bring splinters to the skin's surface. Finely chop cabbage to a mush and place a 1-centimetre thick layer over the skin. Cover with plastic wrap to hold in place.
+ Cabbage water helps relieve **varicose veins** by bringing the blood to the surface of the skin and

allowing it to move around the body faster.

+ Pour cabbage water into a foot bath and soak feet to **relieve aching legs**.

TIP: If you grow arnica in your garden, you can make your own bruise cream. Crush 1 teaspoon of the leaves and stem in a mortar and pestle and add 3 tablespoons of Vaseline or add the ground arnica directly to a small Vaseline container and stir.

SAVE: BREAD

OTHER USES:

+ Make **breadcrumbs**. Place stale bread in the oven on a low heat until it's completely dry but not browned. Crush with the back of a spoon through a sieve or in a food processor. Store the breadcrumbs in a canister in the pantry (the moisture has been removed so they won't go mouldy).

+ Use to make **crostini, croutons or Melba toast**. Cut into the desired shape (cubes for croutons, thin slices for Melba toast). Toast slowly in the oven until golden (5–10 minutes in a fan-forced oven).

+ Use tail ends of white bread to make **modelling clay**. For every cup of mashed white bread add 1 teaspoon of salt and 1 tablespoon of water. Knead it then create any shape you like. Make your own beads. Shape the bread into beads and thread them along a satay stick. Then heat slowly in a fan-forced oven at 130°C (250°F/gas mark 1).

> **TIP:** To make your own wallpaper paste, bring 2 cups of water to the boil and gradually add 1 cup of plain flour and 1 tablespoon of salt. Stir over heat until clear.

SAVE: BRUSSELS SPROUTS

OTHER USES:

+ If you have a **bunion** or bump on the side of your foot or toe, relieve the symptoms with brussels sprouts. Cut one in half, place the cut half on the bunion, bandage in place and leave overnight.
+ Use brussels sprouts tail ends and leaves when making **stocks and soups**.
+ Shred them finely and use in **coleslaw**. Brussels sprouts can always be used as a substitute for cabbage.

SAVE: CARROTS

OTHER USES:

+ Raw carrot gets **rid of roundworms and threadworms** which pass from dogs and cats to humans very easily. Drink a glass of fresh carrot juice each morning for 3 days. Use the same tonic for your pets in their food.
+ Cut a design into them to make a **stamp**.

+ Children can make funny-shaped **vegetable people** from carrots. It's a great way to make eating healthy nibbles more fun.
+ Grow carrot tops in cotton wool (see page 215).

SAVE: CHERRY PIPS

OTHER USES:

+ This is an extreme other use! Use cherry pips to make **Christmas decorations**. After eating the cherries, boil the pips and leave them to dry. While they're still warm, thread each pip through the middle with a heavy darning needle and heavy cotton thread. Paint them with vinyl paint, folk art paints or shellac.

SAVE: COFFEE GROUNDS

OTHER USES:

+ Use as **fertiliser** in the garden. If you don't have a garden, use them as fertiliser in pots containing ferns or rainforest plants. Neighbours might like to use your old coffee grounds in their garden.
+ Add to **compost**.
+ Turn the grounds into **dye**. Add the coffee grounds to water and bring to the boil. Place the item you want to dye in the water until it's the colour you like. Remove the item then transfer to salted water (1 cup of salt for 3 litres of water) to set the dye.

TIP: There's a belief that coffee grounds keep slugs
and snails away from your garden. The grounds
are toxic to slugs and snails but a better way to
keep them away is to mix equal parts sand and
ash and place it around the border of your
garden.

TIP: Buying takeaway coffee every day can add up
very quickly. If you have two coffees a day at
$3.50, that's almost $50 a week or $200 a month
spent on caffeine. And then there's the disposal of
paper cups and lids to consider. If you have your
coffee in a café, you can read the newspaper at
the same time and save $1.30 a day.

SAVE: COOKING OILS

OTHER USES:

+ Most vegetable-based cooking oils can be **reused** as
long as you strain them and remove any food particles.
If you leave used cooking oil on your benchtop, make
sure it's covered so insects can't get in. Store it in a
dripping pot that has a grill and a lid that can be
sealed. Some oils, such as olive, rapeseed and
grapeseed oil have a low smoking point and can't
be reheated too many times because they become
carcinogenic. Peanut, macadamia, avocado and
canola oils are better choices when frying.

+ Old fats and oils can be used to **grease bike chains**. Just make sure there's no floating matter or they will affect the lubrication.
+ **Recycle fats and oils!** Collect used fats in a 5-litre drum and have it picked up by an oil recycler. To find out who collects in your area, ring your local fish and chip shop and find out who collects their old oil.

TIP: To make your own dripping pot, as Shannon has done, use a metallic saucepan with a lid. Cut an old tin can so it makes a second lid and punch holes in the tin in a spiral shape using a small nail, working from the centre of the piece of tin to the outside. This makes the centre of the tin lower to create a funnel so the fat runs to the centre of the grill. To use, pour the used cooking oil onto the grill and any chunky bits will stay on the surface of the tin to be wiped away.

TIP: You can also remove floating matter from oil by using a square of muslin as a strainer. Place the muslin over the mouth of a tin can, secure with a rubber band and pour the oil onto it. Another option is used coffee filters but make sure the oil isn't too hot or it won't work because the coffee filter will collapse. Reuse the oil to make crispy roast potatoes.

? DID YOU KNOW? *In days gone by, people used to collect the fat from cooked meat, render it and reuse it for cooking other meals. The process of rendering involves heating the fat until it's warm but not hot. Then water is added and brought to the boil. It's then left to cool. The proteins sink to the bottom of the pot and the fat hardens on the top. The hardened fat is skimmed off and reused, and the protein soup at the bottom was added to stock. Rendered fat used to be added to face creams!*

? DID YOU KNOW? *Cars that run on diesel can be converted to run on used vegetable oil. You can pick up your fish and chips and fuel at the same time!*

? DID YOU KNOW? *San Francisco operates a service that collects any used vegetable oil from restaurants to recycle into biodiesel. The city expects to save millions because it won't have to unclog water and sewerage pipes blocked by solidified cooking oil.*

SAVE: CUCUMBER

OTHER USES:

+ **Remove dark circles under your eyes** by putting slices of cucumber over them. It brings blood to the surface of the skin.
+ Place cucumber slices on your face to **fade freckles**.

+ Wash cucumbers and peel in broad strips to use as swizel sticks in summer drinks.

 DID YOU KNOW? *You can grow a cucumber into a square shape by putting a square plastic box, such as a takeaway container, around a young cucumber. As it grows, it takes on the shape of the box. Your cucumber will be easy to fit on bread for cucumber sandwiches. At Disney World, cucumbers are grown in the shape of Mickey Mouse.*

WHY IT MATTERS: Australian researchers have found almost three-quarters of Australia's migratory birds have disappeared over the past 25 years. Report author, Professor Richard Kingsford, said the bird populations were in decline because their habitats were disappearing in Australia, Southeast Asia, China and Russia. 'The wetlands and resting places that they rely on for food and recuperation are shrinking virtually all the way along their migration path.'

SAVE: EGGS (NOT ROTTEN)

OTHER USES:

+ Use up excess eggs in **quiches, frittatas and egg wraps** and place them in the freezer. To make egg wraps, combine 3 eggs, 2 tablespoons of self-raising flour, 1 teaspoon of cornflour, 1 tablespoon of milk and a pinch of salt in a bowl and mix well. Add just enough water to make the batter the consistency of thin custard. Pour into a hot frying pan in a thin layer and cook on both sides until just set. Repeat with remaining batter. Place the cooked egg wraps on a sheet of baking paper, store in large zip-lock bags or airtight containers and transfer to the freezer. Thaw and use to wrap around whatever filling you like.

+ Make **lemon meringue pie**. Use egg whites to make the meringue and egg yolks for the lemon butter.

+ Egg white can be used as paper **glue**.

+ Turn egg yolks into **paint**. To do this, mix egg yolks with pigment (available at art supply stores) and olive oil or linseed oil. The amount of each ingredient varies according to the viscosity, opacity and colour you want. Crack an egg, separate the yolk from the white—you must remove all the egg white—and place the egg yolk on some paper towel. Allow the remaining egg white to absorb into the towel. Leave for a day so it's completely removed. Extract the yolk using a syringe. It's what Leonardo da Vinci used for painting!

Fresh eggs from your own chook?

If you have the space, you might like to keep hens and gather fresh eggs. Check with your local council to find out if keeping hens is permitted where you live. In addition to fresh eggs, chooks make great fertiliser and love eating bugs, snails and slugs. Just make sure you buy them from a reputable breeder. When Jennifer was young, the family bought what they thought were hens. They turned out to be roosters. The neighbours weren't happy about the early crowing!

SAVE: EGG SHELLS

OTHER USES:

+ Egg shells are high in calcium, so crush them up and **mix with birdseed**. You won't have to buy shell grit.
+ They are alkaline so crush and **scatter over the garden** on citrus, azaleas, camellias and roses.
+ The next time you make scrambled eggs, **blow the eggshells** and decorate them! To blow eggshells, pierce the top and bottom of an egg with a darning needle. Hold egg firmly and push slowly so you don't break it. Place your mouth over one of the holes and gently blow the egg into a bowl. Rinse the shells thoroughly by using the egg like a straw and sucking water from a bowl to clean out egg residue. Then fill them with warm jelly, place

in the fridge to set and they're ready to decorate.
It's a perfect substitute for chocolate Easter eggs.

 DID YOU KNOW? *Fennel in food or in a tea increases milk production in mothers and helps alleviate mastitis. It also helps reduce wind in babies.*

SAVE: *GARLIC*

OTHER USES:

+ Crush 3 cloves of garlic into a spray bottle and add
  1 litre of water. Allow to steep overnight. Spray over
  plants to **keep snails, slugs, aphids and flying insects
  away**. Don't use inside the house because of the smell.
+ Garlic is a great natural antibiotic and swallowing
  one small piece of garlic like a capsule is a great
  way to stave off colds and flues. It doesn't give
  you bad breath if consumed whole.

SAVE: *HONEYDEW MELON AND ROCKMELON*

OTHER USES:

+ Melons grow very easily. If you have enough
  space, throw pips into the garden and **new fruit**
  will grow. If you grow them over a weedy patch,
  the rapid ground cover will kill the weeds.
+ If you scoop out the fruit from the shell you can use
  the shells as **dessert bowls**. Toss it into your
  compost when you're finished.

SAVE: LEMONS

OTHER USES:

+ Add lemon oil to your broom bristles and sweep spider webs away. You can buy lemon oil or put pantyhose over the head of your broom and scrub a whole lemon over the top. The lemon oil keeps spiders at bay for around 3 months. **Spiders hate lemons**.

+ Use as a **fragrance**. Take the zest of a lemon and allow it to dry on a saucer in the sun for a couple of days. Put 1 teaspoon of dried zest into a spray bottle, add water and allow to steep. Use it to freshen up any room in the house.

+ **Prevent hard water fur and limescale** in your kettle by placing lemon peel inside and boiling. Let it stand overnight and rinse. Do this once a week.

+ Add lemon peel to **washing-up rinse water** to make plates and glasses shine. Don't put lemon peel in the dishwasher because it will cook.

+ Use lemon juice to **whiten clothes**. Add 2 tablespoons of lemon juice to your washing rinse water.

+ Whiten a **wooden breadboard** by scrubbing it with lemon juice. Rub a cut lemon over the surface and leave the breadboard in the sunshine to dry.

+ Use lemon juice to **clean urine stains** from the pipes at the back and grout around the toilet.

+ To **calm an upset stomach** or heartburn, mix the

juice of 1 lemon and ½ teaspoon of bicarb and
drink while fizzing.

+ A glass of hot water with lemon juice, honey and
an aspirin helps **ease a cold**. It's a great source of
concentrated vitamin C.

TIP: To grow your own pineapple, cut off the top
2 centimetres of fruit and the leaves and place
cut-side down in the garden. Pineapples like
tropical conditions but they will grow in most
parts of Australia—the pineapples are smaller
in cooler areas.

DID YOU KNOW? *The Melbourne-based charity One
Umbrella collects unwanted food or food that's close to
its use-by date to make meals for the homeless and
hungry. In 2006 they provided 267,000 meals.*

SAVE: *LETTUCE*

OTHER USES:

+ Most people throw the darker, outside leaves of a
lettuce into the bin. But it can be **lightly braised**
like a vegetable. Wash it clean before cooking or
you might get bits of dirt in your stir-fry.

+ Use the outside leaves of lettuce to **cover food
when heating it in the microwave**.

+ Add chopped to **stocks and soups**.

SAVE: POTATOES

OTHER USES:

+ **Remove rust** from a metal surface by sprinkling a cut potato with coarse salt and rubbing over the rust.
+ **Relieve itching** by rubbing a thin slice of salted raw potato on insect bites.
+ **Darken your hair** or get rid of the brassiness in bleached blonde hair by dipping a comb in water that has been used to boil potatoes. Run the comb through blonde or brown hair several times. Set the colour in the sun.

SAVE: STRAWBERRIES

OTHER USES:

+ Use as a **facemask**. Crush them up, spread over your face and leave for 10–15 minutes. This mask clears blackheads and is great for oily skins. It can also lighten freckles!
+ **Tenderise pork**. Crush strawberries (minus the leaves) and rest in a thin layer over pork for 20 mintues before cooking. Keep the strawberries on when cooking to form a kind of chutney.
+ The leaves on strawberries are a **natural laxative**. If needed, sprinkle in salads like a herb.

TIP: You can freeze strawberries and use them in smoothies, muffins and other meals.

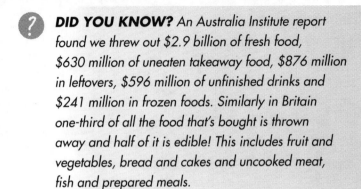

DID YOU KNOW? *An Australia Institute report found we threw out $2.9 billion of fresh food, $630 million of uneaten takeaway food, $876 million in leftovers, $596 million of unfinished drinks and $241 million in frozen foods. Similarly in Britain one-third of all the food that's bought is thrown away and half of it is edible! This includes fruit and vegetables, bread and cakes and uncooked meat, fish and prepared meals.*

TIP: Patronise farmers' and growers' markets. They cut out the middle person bringing fresh produce directly to you. To find one near you, visit www.farmersmarkets.org.au. Support fruit and veg stores or roadside stalls that stock locally grown produce.

DID YOU KNOW? *Even though most people like to get a bargain at the shops, some low prices come at a huge ethical cost. Think about the circumstances that led to the biggest recall of meat in US history. Workers at a slaughterhouse were caught on video torturing 'downer' or sick dairy cows and mixing them in with healthier cows. Not only did this highlight animal welfare issues, a link has been found between downed cattle and mad cow disease. The slaughterhouse was a major supplier of beef to the US National School Lunch Program.*

TIP: Cook excess food and store it in the freezer for those nights when you can't be bothered cooking from scratch. It's cheaper and healthier than getting takeaway.

Stretching your food

Whether it's reheating last night's dinner, making lamb or chicken sandwiches from a roast or cooking bubble and squeak, most households eat leftovers. There are important hygiene issues to be aware of when stretching your food. Never freeze food more than once raw. If it's been frozen raw, it's okay to freeze again once it has been cooked but only once. Once it has thawed, you must cook it. And always put cooked food in the fridge as soon as it has stopped steaming so bacteria won't thrive. This is particularly the case with dairy products. And here's some alarming news if you regularly eat leftover Asian takeaway: you can only keep cooked rice in the fridge for 24 hours because it can harbour a heat-resistant toxin. This also applies to pasta. You can, however, freeze cooked rice or pasta but once thawed, you can only store it in the fridge for 1 day. Only reheat food to boiling point two or three times. Cooked meat (that's well covered) can last for up to 5 days in the fridge.

TIP: Divide and store leftovers in small portions to speed up the cooling process. It also makes reheating a lot easier. Always cover leftover food

in the fridge with plastic wrap or store in an
airtight container so it will keep for longer. Don't
put steaming food in the fridge – allow it to cool
to a tepid temperature to prevent excess bacteria
forming.

How to make five meals from one leg of lamb

We're fortunate that lamb in Australia is grass fed rather
than grain fed—which is better for the environment, and
perhaps tastier for the sheep. Enjoy your lamb for the
remainder of the week with these ideas.

Lamb roast—roast in the oven with vegetables, such as
red onion, parsnip, pumpkin, potatoes and carrot.

Lamb curry—sauté 1 onion, 1 carrot and 3 sticks of
celery. Add 1 cup of diced lamb (or whatever is left
from your roast) with curry paste and brown lamb on
all sides. Dice 4 medium-sized potatoes and 4 medium-
sized tomatoes and add. Cover with water and simmer
until potatoes are tender. Serves 4 people – more if
there's more leftover lamb. Add boiled rice to stretch
the meal.

Lamb fritters—coat slices of roast lamb in flour and
milk and lightly fry until golden.

Shepherd's pie—mince roast lamb in a food processor,
add 2 tablespoons of plain flour mixed with 4 tablespoons of water and add leftover vegetables to the mince.
Place in a casserole dish, add mashed potato to the top

and sprinkle with Parmesan cheese. Cook in preheated 180°C (350°F/gas mark 4) oven for 30 minutes or until golden brown on top.

Lamb soup—throw bones and leftover shards of meat into a large pot and add 1 chopped onion, 2 chopped carrots, 3 sticks of chopped celery and any other vegetables you like. Add ¼ cup of barley and cover with 2 litres of water. For every 600 ml of water add teaspoon of salt and a pinch of pepper. Add a handful of freshly chopped parsley, coriander or celery leaves (don't use dried herbs) and bring to the boil. Reduce heat and simmer until the contents are tender – the longer, the better.

How to make homemade gravy

Before you could buy gravy mixtures from the supermarket, people used to make their own using excess fat and meat juices from a roast. Place 2 tablespoons of cooking juices in a frying pan and add 1 teaspoon of sugar and 1 teaspoon of butter. When the butter melts, add 1 tablespoon of water. Let it bubble and brown, then add 1 tablespoon of plain flour and stir. When the flour has gone clear, gradually add water and continue stirring until you get the consistency you want.

SAVE: JOINTS FROM LEGS OF LAMB

OTHER USES:

+ Turn them into **jacks!** Children used to play jacks, knuckles or onesies using the dried-out joints from legs of lamb. After eating the lamb, wash the knuckle bone and put it on the windowsill to dry, then varnish. You'll need 5 knuckle bones for a decent set.

How to make vegetable stock

Don't throw your vegetable peels away! Use any clean bits of vegetable you'd normally throw out (or wash before you peel) to make vegetable stock. Place 1 kilogram of clean vegetable peels in a pot and add 2 litres of water. Simmer on a low heat until tender (usually two hours). Allow to cool and strain the liquid into an airtight container. Label and keep in the freezer. You can use the tail ends of many vegetables, including mushrooms, carrots, broccoli, cabbage and turnips. The French are renowned for adding to base stocks for years and years!

How to make chicken stock

Keep the carcass of your roast chicken to make chicken stock. Place the carcass in a pot of water and bring to the boil. Simmer for at least 1 ½ hours, strain and store the liquid in a labelled container in the fridge or freezer. If you add a couple of onions and vegies you've got instant chicken soup. Just don't use the bones that people have chomped on!

TIP: Bury chicken bones under exotic plants. They act as a fertiliser like blood and bone.

DID YOU KNOW? *People used to save wishbones from chickens to decorate a church for weddings. The wishbone was dried, painted silver and hung at the end of each pew.*

TIP: To smoke ham or pork bones, place black tea leaves in the base of a frying pan, cover with aluminium foil and pierce the foil with a fork. Place the ham or pork bones on top, cover, turn the frypan to a low temperature and smoke. For every centimetre thickness of meat or bones, smoke for 1 hour. Use the smoked ham or pork bones in pea and ham soup.

DID YOU KNOW? *The University of Sydney's Centre for Integrated Sustainability Analysis has calculated that if we halve our average consumption of meat it would cut the average Australian's greenhouse gas emissions by almost 25 per cent. Cutting out one beef meal a week saves 10,000 litres of water and 300 kilograms of greenhouse pollution a year.*

How to rectify cooking mishaps

What to do if you've added too much salt

Add 1 teaspoon of lemon juice or a couple of slices of apple, which will give the meal a sweet taste.

What to do if you've burnt a meal

If the burn is really bad, throw the meal out and start again: no one likes to eat charcoal. For a mild burn, put 2 slices of bread at the bottom of a cooking bowl and pour the burnt contents on top. This will draw off the moisture and reduce the ashy taste. Ash contains salt so adding something acidic, such as lemon juice or orange juice, will also lessen the ashen flavour.

What to do if you've burnt milk

Remove the scorched taste from burnt milk with a pinch of salt.

What to do if you've added too much chilli

Chilli is an alkali so you can reduce its intensity with acids such as lemon juice, yoghurt, pineapple or vinegar. Casein, the protein in dairy, bonds with the chilli and neutralises it.

What to do if you've added too much sugar

Reduce the intensity of sugar with a squeeze of lemon juice.

What to do if you've added salt instead of sugar to a cake mixture

Turn the mixture into playdough by adding water and food colouring. To prevent it happening again, make sure you label containers well.

CHANGE FOR GOOD: They're becoming more green in the US government. Capitol Hill aims to use electricity generated from renewable sources, install more efficient lighting and move to hybrid and alternative fuel vehicles for all government cars. The privately owned food service, which makes 2.5 million meals a year, will start dishing out local organic seasonal food which can be taken out in compostable containers and eaten with biodegradable utensils.

 DID YOU KNOW? *You can grow mushrooms easily at home. Buy a kit from your nursery.*

How to preserve fruits and vegetables

Fruits and vegetables are tastier and cheaper when in season. But, as we know, they can go off pretty quickly, especially in hot, humid weather. You can dry, stew, glacé, salt, pickle or freeze fruit and vegetables for later use. The process of drying removes moisture so that mould and bacteria can't form. This can be done using the sun, microwave or oven. The important elements are heat, dryness and air circulation.

In the sun

This is the most economical form of drying but you need about 4 really sunny days in a row, which can be hard to predict. If you get rain, take the rack inside and allow to dry for longer. Make (using a wooden box and flywire) or buy a drying rack and cover it in fine-grade mesh so insects can't get inside. Thinly slice the fruit and vegetables, place them on the rack, allowing space for air to circulate, and transfer to a sunny position. The fruit and vegetable slices don't need to be turned because air circulates through the mesh. Bring the rack inside at night. The fruit and vegetables are dried when they are a leathery consistency. Once dried, store in labelled airtight containers in a cupboard and use all year round.

TIP: If drying berries, crush them between two plates to remove as much moisture as possible so they don't rot. Continue this process as they're drying out.

In the microwave

You'll need to buy a specialist microwave drying rack. Place one layer of the fruits or vegetables on a microwave-safe rack and dry according to the manufacturer's directions (the length of time required varies according to the rack and the thickness of the fruits and vegetables). Remove the rack from the microwave and allow to sit for 20 minutes. Wash the rack in boiling water after use.

In the oven

The technique is the same as with the microwave. Place the sliced fruits and vegies on mesh or cake racks and dry in an oven preheated to 70°C (150°F/gas mark ¼) for 1–3 hours, depending on the thickness of the fruit and vegie slices. Don't allow them to brown. Once the fruits and vegetables are dried, they're preserved. Store in a labelled airtight jar or container. They're just like the bought ones!

TIP: To smoke food in the oven, cover a baking tray with 1 centimetre thickness of loose leaf tea under the mesh racks to flavour the food. Cook at 100°C (200°F/gas mark ½) for 1–3 hours. Don't open the oven door until it's completely cooled or your smoke alarm could go off!

How to preserve lemons

Wash whole lemons and place them in a microwave-safe dish with salt and water. For each kilogram of lemons, add 2 cups of salt and enough water to cover. Cover and microwave on high for 4 minutes. Transfer to a container and pack enough salt inside (using your hands) to absorb all the moisture. Seal, label and refrigerate for 3–4 weeks.

TIP: To store oranges, lemons, grapefruits and other citrus fruits for long periods, melt some beeswax until it's just liquified (not too hot) or paraffin wax and pour over the citrus fruit to coat the skin. They will keep like this for 1 month or even longer.

How to glacé

Combine 1 cup of water, 1 cup of sugar and 1 cup of fruit in a pot. Gently bring to the boil over a low heat. When the syrup is clear, the fruit is glacéd. Store in a labelled sterilised jar. Use the juice from the glacé in cooking. Shannon loves using it over a madeira cake. She pours the liquid over the cake, warms it in the oven and the glacé syrup spreads throughout the cake. Yum!

How to make chutney

Combine 1 cup of white vinegar, 1 tablespoon of salt,
2 tablespoons of sugar and 3 cups of water in a large
pot. Add 3 cups of whatever fruits and vegies you like
(it's best to mix equal parts sweet and savoury). Most
chutneys contain stone fruit, such as peaches, apricots,
nectarines or plums. Other choices are tomatoes,
onions, carrots and sultanas. If you want the chutney
to last longer, add an extra 2 tablespoons of sugar and
3 cups of water and cook slowly until reduced to the
desired consistency.

Lounge, Family, Dining Rooms and Study

The durable nature of many of the items in these rooms means we're more likely to care for and pass them on than toss them away. We give heirlooms sentimental and economic value and know it's lovely to have a piece of furniture or ornament that reminds us of family or friends. Of course, there's wear and tear in these rooms but there's also scope for reuse and repair!

A really easy way to save on your electricity bill is to turn appliances off at the power point rather than leaving them on stand-by. The phantom load quickly adds up!

SAVE FEATURE: If you damage a china plate, cup or ornament and it's not worth repairing (if in doubt, check with a restorer), smash it into small pieces and create a mosaic. One idea is to use the fragments of china as a mosaic to decorate a fruit bowl (it won't work on glass bowls). Apply tile glue to the outside of the bowl then stick the pieces into place. Allow to dry then apply grout. All grout is different so follow the directions on the packet. Remove excess grout with a damp sponge before it's completely dry.

TIP: Keep all your broken ceramic bits in a busy box ready to use on a rainy day. To make a busy box, take a container, such as a fruit box or shoebox, and fill it with odds and ends suitable for crafts and repairs. Encourage your friends to do the same. Why meet for just coffee when you could be sitting around a table and creating something together?

The lounge and family rooms

Couches and armchairs

Couches and armchairs should last a long time but there are vulnerable areas, such as the arms. The best way to protect them is with armrest covers. If you don't have them already, have some made or make your own. Use contrasting or matching fabric: they can be made to fit snugly so you can't even tell they're there! If the fabric on your couch has become dated or is worn through, have it recovered professionally or do it yourself. If your couch or cushions have faded in the sun, removable fabric covers can be dyed to look brand new or you can even have a fitted cover professionally dyed!

SAVE: USED COUCHES

OTHER USES:

If the couch is in reasonable condition, contact a charity such as The Salvation Army (www.salvosstores.salvos.org.au), St Vincent de Paul (www.vinnies.org.au) or The Smith Family (www.thesmithfamily.com.au). If the couch has had it, you may be able to reuse some parts of it, such as:

+ **Furnishing fabric** tends to be strong and very durable. The fabric on the outside back of the couch, which has been protected from wear and tear, can be used to make cushion covers.

+ **Cushions** make great buffers, so put them in the back of your car to have on hand when packing or carting delicate items. They could also come in handy to sit on when changing a tyre! You could also re-cover the cushions and keep them in the playroom to use as floor cushions and for making cubbyhouses. Tack a cushion to the top of a wooden chest to make a storage seat. Refashion the sponge and use in pillows. Cut the sponge into blocks to put in your car cleaning kit; it's particuarly good when washing the car. They also make great pet beds.

+ **Springs** can go in your toolbox. Use as a replacement if another spring breaks (or use them as a document sorter or letter rack).

+ **Timber** tends to be of good quality so hold on to it for another use. Create what Shannon calls a lumber pile in your backyard or shed with a stack of timber you can use for another purpose.

+ **Castors** are expensive to buy so hang on to them. You could use them to make a trolley or to go on the base of small bookcases. Store them with other used-hardware items, such as screws. Keeping a collection of odds and ends in your garage or shed saves money and the older versions are often of better quality.

How to make your own trolley

A trolley is particularly handy if you live alone as it makes moving items or rearranging furniture so much easier. Why lug a heavy bookcase when you can roll it on a trolley instead? To make one (it's just like a large skateboard), secure four castors to each corner of a strong piece of 2-centimetre thick marine ply (5 ply). Make sure it's narrow enough to fit through a doorway.

TIP: If your leather couch has seen better days, use the leather backing to strengthen other leather items, such as handbags, or use for patching. Make leather shoelaces using a ruler and a sharp knife. Reinforce a backpack by lining inside the base with a piece of leather. Use it to make handles for baskets. Make patches for the elbows of a favourite jacket or jumper or you could patch the knees of gardening overalls. Leather is perfect for an apron because it's easy to wipe down and is heat resistant. Use leather on shovel handles. Keep a strip of leather in your workshop to use for sharpening knives. Leather also makes a great work surface because it's robust and non-slip. Make a new belt and glue or use a stud to hold the buckle in place.

How to make a throw-cover

Fitting a throw-cover is a cost-effective and relatively easy way to freshen up the look of a couch or armchair. You'll need some lightweight sheeting material, which you can buy in a range of colours and designs, and upholstery twist pins. With a tape, measure the length of the couch from the ground underneath the arm, over the arm and across the seat to the other arm, over the second arm and down to the ground. Add an extra 10 centimetres to each end. To measure the width, start from the centre front of the couch at the ground and measure along the seat, onto the back of the seat, over the back and down to the ground. Add an extra 10 centimetres to each end. As a general rule of thumb, a single bed sheet will cover a small armchair and a king-sized sheet will cover a large couch.

STEP 1: Remove the cushions.

STEP 2: Place the material over the front of the couch with the top draping over the back and the bottom edge touching the floor.

STEP 3: Go to the back of the couch and pull the fabric from either side of the couch together. Tie it in a knot at the centre back of the couch or use an ironing board cover tightener. Then pull the fabric from the top of the couch to stretch down the back of the couch. Fix this fabric to the back bottom corners and centre back of the couch with upholstery twist pins.

STEP 4: Smooth your hand along the material so it sits against the couch and press it into the

crevices at the back and sides of the seat. Make the material as taut as possible. Then fix each corner of the material to the seat base with an upholstery twist pin to hold the section firm.

STEP 5: Smooth any folds at the sides and around the couch into pleats and fix with upholstery pins. Tuck excess fabric under the base of the sofa and secure with upholstery pins.

STEP 6: Cover cushions by placing them in the centre of a length of the fabric. Tie two diagonal corners of fabric into a flat knot. Then tie the remaining two diagonal corners into a flat knot. To make a flat knot, hold your foot over the knot while you tie it so it stays flat.

STEP 7: Replace the cushions. Make any adjustments.

STEP 8: Enjoy your newly covered couch!

SAVE: COFFEE TABLES

OTHER USES:

+ **Repaint** if it's made of timber. Don't forget to sand it first and between coats.
+ Select a theme for your coffee table and **decoupage** it with holiday photos, movie stubs, postcards or any other paraphernalia. Glam it up with some gold leaf (available at art supply stores). Lay out your design on the tabletop and when you're happy with it carefully put it aside. Mix equal parts PVA glue and water in a

container and spread it over the tabletop. Then fix your new design on top. Leave it to dry then brush the glue mixture over your design. To make it waterproof, use spray enamel to finish.

+ **Add a glass top.** Have some glass cut to the same size as the tabletop—a glazier can do this for you. Because it's sitting on a firm surface the glass doesn't need to be toughened but the edges need to be smoothed so people don't cut their fingers. Place pressed flowers or photos underneath the glass for decoration and change them as the mood takes you.

+ **Make a shelf** from a light coffee table. Cut the table lengthways down the middle with a saw and sand the edges. Fix both halves, one above the other, to a load-bearing wall with brackets. Make sure the brackets are strong enough to hold the weight of the newly made shelves.

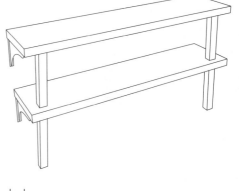

+ Change the legs and turn your coffee table into a **tall table or hallstand**. Buy new legs from a hardware store or second-hand store. Screw them in or bracket them on.

+ **Make an instant table**. Remove the legs from your coffee table and store them separately from the tabletop. When you need a table, rest the tabletop on the legs, two trestles or ottomans. This is great if you are having a party and need a table for drinks. If short on space, store the tabletop behind other furniture or hang it from a wall.

+ For an extreme idea, fix castors to each corner of the top of the table and turn the table upside down. Wind string or rope around the legs to **create a box** that can be wheeled around.

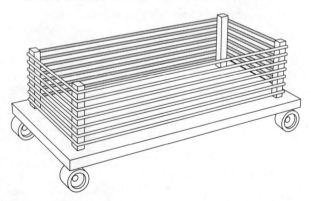

SAVE: MAGAZINES

OTHER USES:

+ Australians love reading magazines! **Before buying a pile of them**, why not organise with

friends to buy particular ones and share them. Magazines are also available to read at your local library.

+ Cut out your favourite pictures, have them laminated and use as placemats. Or paste images you like on cork placemats—this was a very popular trend in the 1980s. For instructions on how to do this, see page 122.

+ Use images for **decoupage**.

+ Cut out images and use them to cover children's **school books**.

+ **Donate** the magazines to a local doctor's surgery or health clinic.

+ Make a **bedside step** for children by taping magazines together with bookbinder tape. It's very solid and won't tip over.

+ Turn old magazines into a **wastepaper bin**! Roll each page of the magazine into a tight tube and apply PVA glue to the edge. Allow to dry. Use some sturdy cardboard and cut it into a circle to form the base of the bin. Using a craft knife, make incisions in the cardboard base for each tube to go into and secure

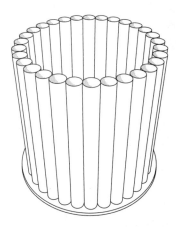

with a dab of glue. Glue the tubes side by side. Once the tubes have been arranged, paint the entire piece with a layer of shellac.

SAVE: OTTOMANS

OTHER USES:

+ Use as **side tables**.
+ Place a large tray on top of the ottoman and use it as a **coffee table** or as a display for books and magazines.
+ If the ottoman is fraying or shabby, cover with a **slipcover**.

SAVE: TRAYS

OTHER USES:

+ **Make a stable table**. Cut fabric 10 centimetres larger than the size of the tray. Then use a hot glue gun to fix gathered fabric (you could use fabric from your rag bag) to the underside edges of the tray, leaving an opening on one side. Pour beanbag pellets into the opening until it's half full and use the hot glue gun to glue the opening closed. The beanbag pellets will mould to the shape of your legs when you rest the tray on top.
+ **Revamp** and cover a wooden tray in fabric, tea towels, cloth serviettes or doilies. Spread PVA glue on top of the tray with a paintbrush, stretch the fabric over

the glue and secure tightly on each corner with a drawing pin. Set aside to dry and then remove the drawing pins. To make it waterproof, paint PVA glue on top of the fabric and allow to dry. You may also like to re-cover the tray with coins, wallpaper, greeting cards, old tickets, paint or spray paint.

Insulation

One of the easiest ways to save up to 40 per cent on your energy costs is to insulate your house. In winter, you want to keep the warm air inside but in summer, you want to keep it out. You'd be surprised how a little gap in your floorboards or under your doors and windows can affect the temperature in a room, so check for draughts. Vulnerable areas are around doorways and windows and under skirting boards. If the door fit is loose, place a felt strip along the jamb. Add a draught brush along the bottom of the door or use a draught stopper or snake. Look at vents and if too much air is getting in (or out), place a special cover over them. Block unused chimneys. (To make a chimney cleaner, place a piece of steel wool on the end of the coathanger and twist it over. Continue adding steel wool until it's 30 centimetres long.) In summer, create breezeways and cross ventilation so cool air can flow through the house. Another thing to be mindful of is heat transference through glass: use curtains or blinds to cover windows. Also check for cracks in external walls and seal them. One way to boost insulation is to use your ceiling cavity to store non-flammable materials.

TIP: If you rent, place heavy pieces of furniture along exterior walls. It keeps the place warmer or cooler. Put extra rugs on floors and hang an additional set of curtains along windows.

TIP: A well-insulated home can be 7°C warmer in winter and 10°C cooler in summer.

Heaters

There are a range of heating options and what you choose will depend on how big your home is, how many people live there and how often the heater is used. All heating (except for solar) creates emissions, so do your homework first. The most energy efficient heating source, after sunshine, is reticulated natural gas. Air-blown or reverse-cycle heaters will run more efficiently if you clean the filter. And, of course, save money by keeping the doors closed in the rooms being heated.

We're afraid there aren't many other uses for old heaters. Many councils collect old ones or you could call a scrap metal recycler. Find one in the *Yellow Pages* or visit www.recycling-nearyou.com.au. Steel is 100 per cent recyclable.

CHANGE FOR GOOD: Many organisations are working towards being climate neutral. For instance, the Sydney Opera House has bought accredited GreenPower and offsets the electricity, audience and performer transport and other emissions from events.

Fireplaces

There's an ongoing discussion about whether open fires are more polluting than electric heaters, particularly when you consider the emissions from coal-powered electricity generators. There's also the issue of whether firewood is sourced from a sustainable supplier (to find one, go to www.firewood.asn.au). Slow-combustion fires are another choice or, if you love the look of an open fire, you can buy ethanol-fuelled fires which are 90 per cent energy efficient and emission-free.

If you do have an open fire, make sure the flue is operating properly or you'll lose a lot of the heat. You'll need professional help to change your flue.

TIP: Ash from a fireplace is alkaline and can be reused in the garden to fertilise and keep snails and slugs away. Ash can also be used to clean stains on the fireplace. Make a slurry using equal parts ash, bicarb, white vinegar and water and

apply with a pair of pantyhose. Always wear
gloves because it's harsh on skin.

TIP: If you have a fireplace, use gumnuts for kindling
because they're dense, dry and burn for a long
time with minimal smoke.

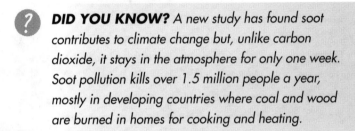

DID YOU KNOW? *A new study has found soot
contributes to climate change but, unlike carbon
dioxide, it stays in the atmosphere for only one week.
Soot pollution kills over 1.5 million people a year,
mostly in developing countries where coal and wood
are burned in homes for cooking and heating.*

SAVE: CURTAINS
OTHER USES:

+ The average curtain is 2½ times larger than the
window it decorates which leaves a lot of fabric
for **recycling**. If you don't reuse your curtains, take
old ones to The Salvation Army, St Vincent de Paul
or The Smith Family. You never know, someone
might be inspired by *The Sound of Music* where
thrifty and capable Maria turned curtains into play
clothes for the children.

+ Cotton muslin and cotton net curtains can be
reused. Cut them into squares, wash in boiling
water to sterilise and dry on the clothesline. The

squares make a fine **sieve** for straining liquids. Use the squares to **cover food** and keep flies away when eating outside. Wrap and secure the squares around several grapes, watermelon or orange slices to feed babies or young children. They can suck on the fruit without swallowing the skin or pips which they could choke on. Just make sure the fruit bundle is the size of a small orange so they can't swallow the whole lot.

+ Heavy fabrics can be turned into **tablecloths, throws, cushion covers or drop sheets**.

Cooling

Many homes now have air conditioners that use a lot of electricity. When buying one, look for the energy efficiency star rating. To help it run efficiently, install it on the shady side of the building. Check the temperature after it's been on for half an hour: 18–21°C is the ideal range for a room in winter and 23–26°C is the ideal range in summer. If you know it's going to be a hot day, turn the air conditioner on early because it works more efficiently when the air is cooler. When it's on, keep windows and doors closed and draw curtains and blinds to reduce heat transfer. Adjust the louvres upwards when cooling and downwards when heating because hot air rises. And make sure you clean the filter regularly.

Fans should be positioned to maximise airflow. They'll also run more efficiently if you clean the blades regularly with a damp cloth. Don't attempt to clean a fan when it's turned on!

TIP: Capture the water from your air-conditioning unit with a bucket. It's filtered and distilled making it perfect to use in your car or iron.

TIP: We don't recommend you repair electrical items yourself because it can be very dangerous. Take them to a repairer. If it can't be fixed, your repairer might like to use it for parts or recycle it. Consult the *Yellow Pages* or go to www.recyclingnearyou.com.au to find the nearest scrap metal recycler. Some will even come to you and remove your old equipment.

TIP: Air conditioners contain copper, aluminium and steel which can be recycled.

Lighting

Around the world, incandescent light bulbs are being phased out in favour of more energy efficient ones. The common replacement is compact fluorescent light bulbs (CFLs) which use a quarter of the electricity of incandescent bulbs and can last up to ten times longer.

Jennifer's council organised for all her globes to be changed to CFLs for free! CFLs are available in bright white or warm white with the latter being more suitable for living rooms and bedrooms. There is one hitch at the moment because CFLs contain mercury so you can't just throw used ones in the bin. Instead, consult your council to find out where the nearest recycling facility is to you. Low energy halogen downlights are now available in Australia. LEDs (light-emitting diodes) are another globe option and can give over 100 lumens per watt. Find out which type suits your lighting needs.

TIP: Clean your globes regularly because dust affects the brightness and energy efficiency of the light.

SAVE: LAMPSHADES

OTHER USES:

+ Lampshades can be **recovered**. Do it yourself or see a professional.
+ Turn into **wastepaper bins**. Weave raffia along the base and sides.
+ Add a base and a handle and turn the lampshade into a **basket**.
+ Put in the kids' play box for

dress ups. Create space helmets from round lampshades: cover with aluminium foil and cut out a spot for the face. To make a diving helmet, cover with copper-coloured paper and draw nuts and bolts on the front.

+ Make Tiffany shades into **fruit bowls**. Turn the lamp upside down, remove the bulb part and weave the open section with raffia, plastic packing strips or leather.

CHANGE FOR GOOD: Many artists now use recycled elements in their work. One art and design shop only sells items that are recycled or 50 per cent sustainable. Circuit boards have been turned into lamps and old dominoes have become bracelets.

Entertainment systems

Australians love their high-tech gadgets. A look at recent sales of plasma and LCD televisions gives an idea of just how much. But you might be surprised to learn these new televisions are a big contributor to greenhouse gas emissions because the bigger screen uses more power. Shannon worked out LCDs use 45 per cent less power than a plasma screen.

DID YOU KNOW? Choice *magazine found that a Sony Playstation3 costs five times as much to run as an average size fridge, or $250 per year.*

When appliances are on stand-by mode they are still a source of emissions. According to the Australian Greenhouse Office, 5–10 per cent of household electricity is used by appliances left on stand-by mode or what's known as the 'phantom load'. To save money and emissions, switch electronic appliances off at the power point. Some manufacturers have attempted to address this and have reduced the stand-by power usage from 20 watts per hour to less than 1 watt per hour.

 DID YOU KNOW? *According to Choice magazine, if you have a desktop computer, LCD monitor, wireless router, plasma TV and DVD player on continuous active standby it could add $450 per year to your electricity bill.*

One of the more frustrating issues with electronic goods is what to do with them once you've finished with them. Walk along any street at council clean-up time and you're guaranteed to see many old TVs and stereos sitting on the nature strip. There have been calls for Extended Producer Responsibility Schemes where manufacturers take on the cost and responsibility of recycling. Even though it's likely the cost would be passed on to the consumer, it would be preferable to electronic goods ending up in landfill. The industry is currently working on the best approach. Planet Ark has an online service which links to recycling facilities in your area at www.recyclingnearyou.com.au.

 DID YOU KNOW? *One reason to be concerned about TVs in landfill is the lead content in cathode ray tubes. Lead is harmful when ingested.*

 TIP: Plasma and LCD screens are very delicate so take care when cleaning them. Make sure they are turned off and cool, use a lint-free cloth (don't use paper towel) and don't apply pressure. Some can handle mild soap but not all, so consult the manufacturer's manual. If using a spray, apply to a lint-free cloth rather than spraying directly onto the screen.

 DID YOU KNOW? *The advent of plasma and LCD screens means large entertainment units are no longer popular. Jennifer tried to sell her old one online and no one was interested in buying it. Second-hand dealers told her they just don't sell anymore because people prefer low-lying shelving units. Shannon has turned an old entertainment unit into storage in the garage.*

SAVE: *OLD CDS AND DVDS*

OTHER USES:

+ **Deter bats and birds** by hanging CDs from trees. Birds don't like sharp movements or sunlight reflecting from the CDs.

+ Use as drink **coasters**. Paint a line around the outside edge so you don't mix them up with the CDs and DVDs you still use.

+ Turn CDs into **earrings**. Put old CDs in a bowl of boiling water to soften them and, wearing protective gloves, cut into decorative shapes with tin snips. While the cut CD is still hot, twist it to make earrings. If CDs are cut cold, the edges are as sharp as glass, so be careful. If cut hot, the edges soften. Smooth any sharp edges with a sapphire nail file.

+ Glue several CDs together to make a **sculpture**. Or make a disco ball: cut CDs into small shapes and glue the pieces over a *Styrofoam* craft ball.

+ Make a funky **hanging room divider**. Join several CDs together along a line with fishing wire. Suspend from some dowel or an old broom handle and hang from the ceiling.

SAVE: *VINYL RECORDS*

OTHER USES:

+ Many old vinyl records have become **collectables** so check if your collection has any value by looking online or visiting a second-hand record shop.

+ Old records can be melted in the oven and reshaped into **bowls** or pot plant holders. To do this, put the vinyl on top of some aluminium foil and place it over an ovenproof bowl. Cover the other side of the vinyl in aluminium foil and place in a preheated 150°C (300°F/gas mark 2) oven. When the vinyl begins to melt, shape it over the bowl using a wooden spoon (so you don't burn your fingers) and allow to cool. Either cork the hole at the bottom or use it as a drain.

+ Cut old vinyl records in half, punch holes along the cut edge and thread with string, old shoelaces or ribbon and use as covers for **photo albums**.

TIP: Use old record turntables to display art. Cover the base of the turntable with white or black velvet and place the artwork on top. You can show your work of art from all sides.

SAVE: RUGS AND CARPET

OTHER USES:

+ Carpet is easy to cut and reshape with a utility knife or shears. Use in the **garage or workshop** on the workbench to stop small items from bouncing. Or wrap cut strips around handles to give a better grip.

+ Turn old carpet into **rugs**. You can have the edges professionally sealed. Contact a carpet manufacturer or retailer.
+ Cut carpet into usable squares and place under other items, such as the feet of furniture to **protect the floor** from scratches.
+ Use as a front or back **doormat**. Cut carpet into squares and tape the edges with iron-on fabric tape. Have them stacked in a convenient place, such as under the bed, ready to use when needed.
+ Use as a **door seal**. If the door is rattling, glue a strip of carpet down the doorjamb.
+ Go all Mary Poppins and make a **carpetbag**. Cut out a piece of carpet, fold it in half and stitch around the side edges with a large bodkin needle. Make sure you wear gloves because the carpet is hard on your hands and you may have to use a small pair of pliers to pull the needle through the carpet. Either make a cloth handle or buy screw-on handles from your local craft store.
+ **Wrap rafters** or exposed beams in carpet to cushion the blow if you bump your head. Use in areas away from view, such as under the house or in the garage, because it doesn't look very attractive.
+ Turn into a **trivet or pot stand**.

+ Carpet takes dye very well so it's easy to paint. Paint a design on carpet or a rug and **hang** it on the wall for insulation or decoration.

+ Use a carpet square as a base for **beading or electrical work**. Your tiny pieces won't bounce onto the floor.

+ **Protect table surfaces** by placing old carpet cut to size on top when the kids are playing or decorating.

+ Cut carpet into sections and place it over your garden beds to **control weeds**. It will rot and keep the weeds down.

+ If you have hessian-backed wool carpet, wrap it around your hot water pipes for **insulation**. Don't use nylon or nylon-backed carpet because it will melt.

+ Put carpet in the base of a **toolbox**. Any rust and grease can be shaken from the mat easily. It also helps absorb moisture so your tools don't rust.

+ Use extra carpet squares on the floor of your **car**. The carpet in cars is expensive and wears easily.

TIP: To save money, cut the end off a full vacuum cleaner bag, discard the contents and seal the bag with painter's tape. Before vacuuming, empty the bag because the machine will work more efficiently. It's a good idea to regularly vacuum your carpet because dirt breaks the fibres down and increases the wear.

SAVE: *PINE CHRISTMAS TREES*
OTHER USES:

+ We all love a gift that keeps on giving, which is exactly what a pine Christmas tree can do. When the season of goodwill slips into Epiphany (or when the needles all fall off) take your Christmas tree outside, place it on the ground and run a garden rake along the trunk to strip the needles from the tree. Use the pine needles as **mulch** for gardenias, camellias, citrus, azaleas and Australian natives.

+ But wait, that's not all this tree can give. Turn the thin branches into a **wreath**. To do this, cut the branches with secateurs so that they fit into a bucket and soak in hot water for 2 hours. Weave the branches into a wreath for next Christmas. It will give off a lovely pine smell.

+ Turn the trunk into a **doorstop**. Saw off a small wedge-shaped section from the bottom of the tree and place it under a door. Write the date and a message on the cut edge with permanent pen or a soldering iron. The remainder of the trunk can be cut into sections and placed in hot water. Rub any rough or knotty bits with steel wool or sandpaper and leave to dry. Use them as **candle supports**. Put the remaining branches in the **lumber pile** to use as **firewood**.

SAVE: *CHRISTMAS LIGHTS*

OTHER USES:

+ The wire can be removed from Christmas lights
  and cut into short lengths. Use for **tying** things,
  such as plants, in the garden.

> ? **DID YOU KNOW?** *If replacing skirting boards, avoid
> ones made of fibreboard (MDF) because it contains large
> amounts of adhesives and formaldehyde which aren't
> good for your health. Avoid expensive timber skirting by
> buying recycled ones.*

The dining room

A dining table is a true workhorse. It can be a meeting place for family and friends and can also double as a homework and study table. The table will last longer if you wipe up any spills as soon as you can and use a table protector, tablecloths, placemats and coasters.

SAVE: DINING TABLE

OTHER USES:

+ If the dining tabletop is broken, try to **repair** it. Fit another one using particle timber, an old timber door, recycled timber or use a second-hand tabletop. You can have them cut to size at the hardware store.

+ Old dining tables can become **office desks**. If the legs are cumbersome, remove them and use a filing cabinet or a chest of drawers at either end as support.

+ **Hold on** to useful timber and place it in what Shannon calls a 'lumber stack'.

TIP: If you get a water mark on a timber tabletop, work out what the table has been sealed with: varnish, polyurethane, shellac or wax. To do this, take a pin or needle, hold it in a pair of pliers and heat it on the stove. Touch the pin or needle to an inconspicuous part of the table and smell the fumes it creates. If it smells like burnt plastic, it's polyurethane. If it smells like an electrical fire, it's an oil-based varnish. If it smells like burnt hair, it's shellac. If it smells like a snuffed candle, it's waxed. To repair polyurethane, apply a little Brasso with a lint-free cloth and rub swiftly over the mark in the direction of the grain. It will look worse before it looks better! Brasso partially melts polyurethane and allows it to refill the tiny air holes that create the white mark. Shellac, varnish and wax can be repaired using beeswax. Warm beeswax in a bowl in the microwave until it just softens and apply with the back of a piece of lemon peel (yellow side). Rub in the direction of the grain using speed, not pressure.

SAVE: TIMBER DINING CHAIRS

OTHER USES:

+ If the chairs are in good condition, sell or donate them to a charity.
+ Turn **cushions** from dining chairs into **kneeling pads** for gardening.
+ Screw the dining seat to a strong box on castors to make a small, wheeled **stool** for the garden. It makes weeding easier and you can store tools inside the box.
+ Dismantle the chairs and keep the timber. Store in

a neat pile or **lumber stack**, as Shannon calls it.

+ Keep dowel from chairs. Turn into **coat hooks** for the back of a door, use as replacement handles on gardening tools or make into doorstops.

TIP: Turned timber is always wanted at timber recyclers. Check online to find one near you.

SAVE: *TABLECLOTHS*

OTHER USES:

+ If your tablecloth is wearing thin, convert it into **serviettes**. If you don't have a sewing machine, use iron-on hem binding which comes in a range of colours.

+ Make aprons or **work shirts**. Shannon turns them into smocks for her workshop.

+ Save for **patching** or for the rag bag.

TIP: If your serviettes are permanently stained, dye them a shade darker. Use hot water dye or the colour will leach when washed at a later stage.

SAVE: *SIDEBOARDS*

OTHER USE:

+ Add shelving to create a CD and DVD **storage unit**.

SAVE: CORK PLACEMATS

OTHER USES:

+ **Repair** them. If the images are beginning to fade on your cork placemats, apply new ones. Remove the old label by soaking it in a tray of hot water with a little dishwashing liquid. Allow the cork to dry. Select a new image (from magazines, wrapping paper, etc). Apply equal parts PVA glue and water to the back of the new image and lay it over the cork. Press a rolling pin or bottle over the top to remove any bubbles. Set aside to dry.

+ If the entire set is no longer viable, use the cork under **table legs** and **chair legs** so they don't scratch the floor. Use scissors to cut the cork to size.

+ Cut to fit under your **vases** to prevent watermarks.

+ Use as **heat-resistant mats** in the kitchen.

SAVE: CANDLE ENDS

OTHER USES:

+ Melt wax ends together to make a **new candle**. Either use a new wick or a wick from an old candle.

+ Add to the **kids' art box** and use for wax-resist paintings or carving.

+ When sewing a button on a suit, **wax the thread** first to make it stronger and to hold the fibres of the thread. Drag the thread over the candle end.

+ Wipe sewing needles over a candle stub to **prevent rust** and make sewing smoother.
+ Smooth a candle over the runners on **sticky drawers** to stop them from jamming.
+ **Fill holes** in marble or granite. Warm the wax, drip it into the hole, smooth the excess with a pair of pantyhose then use a hair dryer over the top for a slick, flush finish.
+ Use to **waterproof fabrics**, such as aprons. Warm the wax, dip a scrap of fabric in it and rub it over the entire area.
+ Use as an **alternative to silicone** to seal between the sink and splashback in the kitchen.

TIP: To make candles last longer and drip less, put them in the freezer for a couple of hours before using them. To reduce the size of the flame and amount of sooty smoke, trim the wick to as low as 4 mm.

How to make flowers last longer

Fresh flowers will last longer if you cut the stems just before putting them in water. Maintain the water level by adding ice cubes to the vase every morning and night. Chilled water also helps flowers last longer. Add 1 teaspoon of bleach or 1 aspirin to the vase water to prevent bacteria. Use the sachets supplied by florists.

TIP: For lily pollen, turmeric, curry powder, nicotine or any yellow pollen stains, apply lavender oil. On hard surfaces, use 1 teaspoon of lavender oil per litre of water and wipe with a cloth or sponge. On fabric, apply a couple of drops of straight lavender oil, rub with your fingers and rinse with water.

How to make your own potpourri

There are a couple of ways to make potpourri. One is to place flower petals (any fragrant petal is fine) in a bowl and turn them each day until they dry out. The other way is to dry them in the microwave. Lay the flower petals on a sheet of paper towel and heat them in 30-second bursts until dry. Add 1 teaspoon of orris root powder to an ice-cream container of dry petals and the potpourri can last up to 12 months. Otherwise, it will last for 6 months. Don't use daisies because the dried petals smell like cat urine!

SAVE: *SILVERWARE*

OTHER USES:

+ Turn an old teapot into a **vase** or grow a pot plant in it.
+ Use teapots as **watering cans** for pot plants inside the house.
+ Put teapots on display or use as **decoration**.

TIP: Don't throw old silver away. It can be sold, melted down and turned into other silver items. Merchant jewellers buy and sell old silver and pay by the ounce.

SAVE: SUGAR BOWLS
OTHER USES:
+ Store **cotton balls** in them.
+ Fill with **talcum powder** and place a powder puff on top.

SAVE: SERVIETTE RINGS
OTHER USES:
+ Use to **tie back curtains**. Attach to the wall with Velcro spots.
+ Use as a **toggle for scarves**.

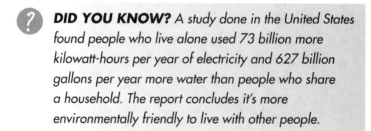

DID YOU KNOW? *A study done in the United States found people who live alone used 73 billion more kilowatt-hours per year of electricity and 627 billion gallons per year more water than people who share a household. The report concludes it's more environmentally friendly to live with other people.*

SAVE: LIQUEUR BOTTLES
OTHER USES:
+ Remove the labels and use as **vases or decorative pieces**. Use several along a window to obscure

an unattractive view without blocking the light.

+ Fill with **bubble bath**. For an easy recipe, see page 172. It's a great gift idea.

+ Use mini-liqueur bottles to **store salad dressing** when taking lunch to work or school.

SAVE: DOILIES

OTHER USES:

+ If you don't have any doilies, you can always find them at second-hand and charity stores. Use them to **protect furniture**.

+ Place them **over jugs** to keep flies away.

+ Stitch onto **an apron to make pockets**.

+ Sew onto **cushions** for decoration.

+ Fold a doily in half and stitch along the edge leaving an opening. Fill with potpourri, stitch closed and place in **wardrobes and drawers**.

+ Make a **fancy evening skirt** for a Barbie doll.

+ Sew doilies onto the **edges of hand and bath towels** for decoration. (See *How to be Comfy* for detailed directions.)

+ Stitch doilies together to make a **table runner**.

TIP: You can sell antique linen to vintage stores. There's been a revival in people making heirloom clothes from antique linen.

The study

The paperless office hasn't quite arrived but we're certainly more conscious of how we use and recycle paper. Thanks to the internet, email, disk drives and memory sticks, more information can be kept virtually which helps to save trees.

You can put some money-saving strategies into place in the study by having a good organisational system for bills and payments so you avoid late fees. One way to keep on top of bills is to enter the details on internet banking as soon as the bill arrives but select the 'payment by' option and enter the date when the bill is due. It means the money stays in your account until the very last moment but the bill is paid on time.

Computers

Computers and printers are getting cheaper to buy but there's still confusion about what to do with old ones. In Australia, around 1.6 million computers are dumped in landfill each year. Then there's a staggering 5.3 million old computers collecting dust at people's homes. HP and Dell recycle old computers (Dell will come to your home and pick up your old computer for a small fee) and Apple has just started collecting unwanted ones. There are also electronic waste recyclers such as www.ewaste.com.au which charge a fee to remove your old electronics. Another option is to contact your local council to see if they have a recycling service. Groups can be found online who refurbish and pass computers on to disadvantaged groups. You could also check with Planet Ark's www.recyclingnearyou.com.au to find out your nearest recycling centre. Just make sure you remove any sensitive information from the hard drive before you pass your computer on. Disk-cleaning software is available for this purpose or you could physically remove the hard disk.

TIP: Don't throw your printer cartridges in the bin. Recycle them in 'Cartridges 4 Planet Ark' bins which can be found at most post offices.

CHANGE FOR GOOD: The state of Victoria runs a system called Byteback which collects and recycles old or broken computers, printers, keyboard cables and power packs. Up to 97 per cent of all material collected through Byteback is recycled.

TIP: You can buy a power board that turns all your computer powered devices on and off so you don't use stand-by power.

DID YOU KNOW? Lots of the components in computers are coated in gold because it's a great electrical conductor that doesn't corrode. Sadly, there's not enough to make it worthwhile to melt down.

Australians love their mobile phones. In 2007, there were 22 million mobile phones being used and their popularity just keeps on rising. Mobile phone batteries contain cadmium and need to be recycled. To find out where to deposit them, check www.mobilemuster.com.au.

 DID YOU KNOW? *Screensavers don't save energy but cycle images so that one image doesn't become burnt on the monitor's screen. This isn't necessary for LCD screens because they don't get image burn.*

How to dispose of batteries

Don't throw your batteries into the bin because it's bad for the environment. Many places recycle them. If you can, use rechargeable batteries. Shannon's husband uses rechargeable batteries and labels them so he knows when they were last charged.

SAVE: *BOOKS AND COVERS*

OTHER USES:

+ **Sell** to second-hand bookshops.
+ **Donate** old books to school libraries or your local library. If they don't want them, they often hold book fairs to raise money.
+ Cut up old picture books for **decoupage**.
+ If there's a favourite poem or piece of text in a book, cut it out, paste it on cardboard and make

a **card** or stick it in a diary or storybook.

+ Some old books have marbled pages. Use these pages to make **gift cards, wrapping paper or bookmarks**. If someone loves Shakespeare, use old pages from a book for their birthday card.

+ Cut out pages and stick them together and use as **drawer liners**. Just make sure the paper is acid free. Books printed before 1950 are acid free.

+ Turn pages into **wallpaper**. You could have an entire wall covered in the pages from your favourite book. Or cover the wall of your loo with old books (seal with clear waterproof finish). You'll always have something to read.

SAVE: OLD TELEPHONE BOOKS

OTHER USES:

+ Save old *Yellow Pages* for **papier-mâché projects**. Make a miniature village using chicken wire and papier-mâché. When water is added, the pages turn green which makes them ideal for creating hills and valleys. You could even sprinkle over some grass clippings.

+ The paper in *Yellow Pages* is perfect to use as a **stencil** to carve designs for screen printing.

 DID YOU KNOW? *Old jewellery boxes were often made of papier-mâché coated in shellac.*

SAVE: OLD GREETING CARDS

OTHER USES:

+ Use in children's **craft projects**. Donate them to daycare centres and preschools.
+ Use old greeting cards to **decorate soap**. Cut out the image you like, dampen the surface of the soap with water and rub the picture onto it with your finger. Make sure you get some of the soap film over the top of the picture to help it stick. Allow to dry.
+ **Frame** cards that you love and use them to decorate your home.
+ Keep them for **decoupage**.
+ Turn old greeting cards into **new cards**. Cut out the images you like and glue them to a new piece of cardboard.
+ **Recycle them**. After Christmas, Planet Ark collects and pulps old cards. It says 600 million cards have been recycled saving over 115,000 trees.

SAVE: WRAPPING PAPER

OTHER USES:

+ There's so much exquisitely designed wrapping paper it seems a shame to throw it out. **Reuse** it! Remove the sticky tape. If it's stuck, place a warm iron on the back of the paper over the sticky tape and the heat should release the glue. While

you're at it, iron the paper ready to use again.
Dress it up with ribbons or string. Combine various
off-cuts to create different effects.

+ **Cover schoolbooks** or journals.
+ Use as **backing on a noticeboard**.
+ Shannon cuts out shapes from old wrapping
  paper and sticky tapes them together to form **new
  wrapping paper**. You can also weave different
  strips of paper to make new sheets.

SAVE: RIBBON

OTHER USES:

+ Turn ribbons into **bookmarks**.
+ Use old ribbon along a bookshelf to **sort books**
  into sections.
+ Sturdy ribbon can be used to **hang paintings** on
  walls.
+ There's always the option of using it to tie over
  little girls' **pigtails**.
+ Reuse to **wrap** around gifts and parcels.

SAVE: CLOCKS

OTHER USES:

+ Most clocks, and this includes digital clocks,
  can be repaired. If they can't, don't throw them
  out because the parts can be used to repair other
  clocks. Take them to a watchmaker.

+ The cogs inside clocks can be made into **jewellery**. Some cogs even have jewels such as sapphires and rubies in them.

DID YOU KNOW? *The Federal parliament is going green. Minimum five-star ratings for government office buildings and leases will become the norm with the most efficient and cost-effective appliances used for Commonwealth operations.*

Bedroom

The bedroom is a reuse haven. Just about everything including bed linen, jewellery, coat-hangers and clothing can be saved or converted for reuse. If searching for inspiration, think about the dress worn by Lizzy Gardiner at the 1994 Academy Awards made entirely from Gold Amex cards! Save money by stocking your wardrobe with clothes that mix and match, find alternative uses for old socks and shoe boxes and keep the room pest free so you won't have to deal with moth-eaten blankets.

SAVE FEATURE: Don't throw old socks away even if they have holes in them. Instead, add them to your cleaning kit. When cleaning venetian blinds, place a sock over your hand, pinch the slat between thumb and forefinger and gently slide along the dusty surface. Cover your hands in old socks when cleaning silverware. You won't transfer oil from your hands to the surface you're cleaning.

Beds

We all know how important it is to have a comfy bed but have you given any thought to environmentally friendly beds? When buying a new one, there are a couple of things to consider. If buying a timber bed, choose one that's been certified by the Forest Stewardship Council (FSC) or buy a second-hand one. Beds made of plastic and polypropylene are not recyclable so avoid them if you can. Be mindful of the material used to make the mattress and avoid those made with polybrominated diphenyl ethers (PBDE) that have been linked with brain and thyroid problems in rats. Instead, look for mattresses made with cotton, wool or hemp. It's worth spending a bit more to get natural materials because it lasts longer and is easier to clean.

TIP: Make sure you air a new mattress well before sleeping on it. This will help to remove any unpleasant odours created in the manufacturing process. If you can, place it in the sun, sprinkle with bicarb and leave for 2 hours. Do this to both sides of the mattress, then vacuum. If you can't get it into direct sunshine, use a UV light.

TIP: Deal with dust mites with used tea bags. Place the used tea bags in a spray bottle of cold water, allow to steep for 5 minutes, remove the bags then lightly mist over the mattress and surrounds. Spray lightly over pillows and dry in the sun.

SAVE: OLD BED
OTHER USES:

+ Turn an old bed into an **indoor or outdoor couch**. For an indoor couch, cover the mattress in a doona cover and add throws and comfy cushions. For an outdoor couch, cover the mattress in plastic (you should be able to get some from shops that sell mattresses) to protect it from rain. Then place an old doona cover over the mattress. Make the doona cover waterproof by taking it outside and spraying it with clear varnish. If there's a frame around the bed, paint it in a bright, weatherproof paint. Pile some cushions on top and you've got a day bed.

TIP: Freshen up your bedhead by painting it a new colour or upholstering it in new fabric.

TIP: Instead of using an electric blanket, sit on a cuddle blanket before going to bed and use it to cover your feet when you get into bed.

SAVE: MATTRESSES
OTHER USES:
+ If your mattress is ripped or torn you can have the cover (the ticking) **replaced**. Search the internet or phone book for a company in your area.
+ Use as a **play base for children**. Put an old doona cover over the top and rest it on the floor. Don't use it if the coils have come through or are rusted or you'll be heading to the emergency department for a tetanus shot!
+ If you want to throw it out, contact a **mattress recycling service**, such as ww.dreamsafe.com.au.

TIP: Your mattress will last longer if you care for it. Rotate it and vacuum it regularly. Put different coloured ribbon on each corner so you know where you are in the rotation cycle.

SAVE: PILLOWS

OTHER USES:

+ Use as **stuffing** for toys or cushions.
+ Use the pillow filling as **packing** when carting a delicate item.
+ Store **in the car** in case someone wants to have a nap.

TIP: Don't forget to wash your pillows at least once every six months (more if you're a heavy sweater). Wash with cheap shampoo in blood-heat water and dry them on top of the clothesline, turning regularly until completely dry.

Bed linen

SAVE: SHEETS

OTHER USES:

+ Turn torn, worn and damaged sheets (and doona covers) into **pillowcases**.
+ Use as a **drop sheet** when painting. The drop sheet will become waterproof the more paint drops you get on it. To speed this process up,

paint the sheet using the tail ends of paint, leave it to dry and you've got a waterproof drop sheet.

+ Turn a double- or queen-sized sheet into a **doona cover** for a single bed. Or sew two single sheets together to make a doona cover. For a reversible look, use different patterned sheets for either side of the cover.

+ Use sheets as **dust sheets** to cover furniture.

+ If having a picnic, put a sheet **under the picnic blanket** to collect dirt. Sheets are easier to wash than blankets.

+ Rip them up and place them in the **rag bag**.

+ The fabric in old sheets is lovely and soft and can be **turned into great pyjamas**.

+ Use old sheets in the **kids' dress-up box**. Turn them into superhero capes or princess trains and dye them the desired colour. Or cut out two holes for eyes and make a ghost outfit.

+ Make a **play rug** (see page 189 in *How to be Comfy* for details).

+ **Create banners or bunting** to hang in a child's bedroom. Paint the sheet with white undercoat and add your design.

+ Use them to **protect and store winter clothes or evening wear**. It's better to wrap clothes in old sheets than leave them in plastic bags because the plastic can leave acid marks. Cut a small hole in the centre of a sheet and poke the hook of a coat-hanger through the hole. Place evening wear on the coat-hanger, cover with the sheet and hang in your wardrobe.

+ Use as a **mat** in the hallway when it's raining.

DID YOU KNOW? *In days gone by, sheets were very expensive to buy so every effort was made to get the most use from them. Sheets tend to wear more in the middle, so they were cut down the centre and the outside hems were stitched together so the inside of the sheet became the outside. By doing this you get twice as much life from the same sheet. The only problem is you then have a seam line running along the centre of your bed – which is why the flat seam was invented!*

How to make your own sheets

Good-quality sheets are still expensive to buy. The higher the thread count, the higher the price. If you're handy with the sewing machine, you can make your own for a fraction of the cost. Find out where your nearest fabric warehouse is in the phone book or online and buy sheeting by the metre. You only need to sew two hemlines on the raw edges or, for those who can't or won't sew, use iron-on hemming tape instead. It's also quite easy to put elastic around a base sheet but you may prefer to keep things simple and make flat rather than fitted sheets. A flat sheet can be used as a top or bottom sheet and will wear more evenly. Shannon also adds cotton lace to decorate her top sheet and is still using sheets made over 15 years ago.

TIP: More energy is needed to make synthetic fibres, so choose cotton or other natural fabrics over synthetic sheets. Cotton also feels much better against your skin and breathes!

Patchwork quilting

Patchwork came about at a time when nothing was ever wasted. Instead of tossing out a frayed shirt, it would be cut into squares and turned into a quilt. And given blankets used to cost the equivalent of several months' wages, there was a financial incentive to turn old clothes into blankets. Some people used to buy sample fabric from door-to-door salesmen at discounted prices, which is why some quilt covers were made from suit fabric. Patchwork quilting is now a popular hobby and many quilts are considered works of art. Quilters also talk about how satisfying it is to see a favourite old skirt, dress or shirt given a new lease of life as a quilt. It keeps the memories alive! Store your patchwork squares in acid-free tissue paper and place them in the centre of old cardboard paper rolls. That way you can easily see which colours you need and the corners of the fabric won't become dog-eared. Why not make patchwork quilting a group experience and sew with your friends?

TIP: Curling under a blanket on the couch is cheaper than turning on the heater and will save on your electricity bill. And if it's a patchwork quilt you've made yourself, you can leave it folded over the sofa for guests to admire.

SAVE: PILLOWCASES

OTHER USES:

+ Keep a pillowcase to use as a **shoe bag** when travelling. That way you won't get dirt on your clothes.
+ **Protect your delicates** when they're being washed in the washing machine by placing them inside a pillowcase.
+ Boil them in hot water, dry them on the clothesline and use them as **ham bags** to keep a leg of ham fresh.
+ Because they're acid-free, they're great to **store winter woollens**.
+ Use them as a **sack for Santa**. Have the kids decorate them.
+ If you've inherited a **fur coat** (it's not environmentally

friendly to buy a new one), use an old pillowcase to clean it. Place 1 kilogram of unprocessed wheat bran (it's abrasive and absorbent) inside the pillowcase, add the coat, secure the top and shake. Then shake off the bran outside and, if necessary, give the fur a light vacuum.

SAVE: BLANKETS/THROWS

OTHER USES:

+ Turn a blanket into a **poncho** to keep you warm in winter. Cut a hole in the middle for your head.
+ Add a length of old blanket to an existing blanket to **make it bigger** and easier to tuck into the side of a bed. Shannon is in the process of doing this with her blankets.
+ Turn them into **cuddle blankets** (see page 204).
+ Cut blankets into strips and wrap them around **wooden beams** where you might bump your head.
+ Wool is a fire retardant, so use old woollen blankets to make **barbecue aprons**.
+ Cut blankets into large squares or rectangles. If making necklaces or beading with children, use these **woollen mats** on the tabletop so the beads won't bounce onto the floor.
+ **Create a new lining** in a lightweight jacket using an old blanket to make a warm winter jacket.

+ Leave an old blanket in the **back of the car** for emergencies. You could even use it to protect the car during a hailstorm.
+ Put them in the toy box to use as cubby house walls.

TIP: The best way to clean blankets is to wash them in a small quantity of cheap shampoo diluted in blood-heat water and rinse them in a small quantity of cheap hair conditioner mixed with blood-heat water. They'll feel lovely and soft.

SAVE: DOONAS

→ Doonas tend to last for a long time. If the filling has become compacted, there are companies that will clean and replace the filling.

OTHER USES:

+ Use the filling inside doonas as **stuffing for toys or cushions**.
+ Turn doonas into **bedding for pets**.
+ Use an old doona as a **mattress protector**.

TIP: Be careful when storing bedspreads. Always wrap them in acid-free tissue paper with naphthalene flakes or camphor balls and store them in a cotton covering. That way they won't be full of moth holes the following winter!

Furniture

SAVE: OLD WARDROBES

OTHER USES:

+ Many old wardrobes are beautiful pieces of furniture. Rather than throwing them away, turn them into a **linen press, computer cabinet, larder in the kitchen or storage in your garage or workshop**.

+ Turn a wardrobe into a **gardening shed**. To do this, turn the wardrobe sideways and fix it to an outside wall. Just make sure the wall and brackets are strong enough to hold it! Attach two chains to the inside ends of the wardrobe door so it sits flat when opened. Attach another chain to the centre of the top wardrobe door. Hook it to the wall to hold it open when using.

+ If the wardrobe is made of timber, the quality is generally very good so reuse the timber to make a **chest or shelving**.

TIP: Revamp an old wardrobe with a new coat of paint or some wallpaper. *Vogue Living* recently showcased a Louis XV walnut armoire spray painted in gaudy colours by graffiti artist KID4EVA.

SAVE: *WIRE COAT-HANGERS*
OTHER USES:

+ Coat-hangers are made with 22-gauge wire so they're easy to manipulate with your hands. Make into a **mobile**.
+ Use them to **hang a mosquito net** above a bed.
+ Make a **butterfly net**. Turn a wire coat-hanger into a hoop and attach net curtaining.
+ Straighten an old coat-hanger and use it to **get behind cupboards** or any tight space.
+ Put old pantyhose over the end and **clean drains** with them.
+ Turn coat-hangers into hooks to **hang handbags**. Open out the coat-hanger, cut it into 3-centimetre lengths and bend into S shapes.
+ Attach a coat-hanger to the fridge and place a couple of pegs along the bottom to **hang children's artwork**. Glue to a magnet or attach using double-sided tape.

+ Hang a 1950s-style fabric **peg bag** or plastic bag
  from it to store pegs.

SAVE: OLD MIRRORS

OTHER USES:

+ Turn into a **tray**.
+ Use behind plants in the **garden** to make the
  space look bigger.
+ Place in the bottom of a wardrobe to **increase the
  light** so you can see into the back. Old mirrors
  are great anywhere it's dark. You can even put
  one at the bottom of a handbag so you see what's
  inside (although it might look as though you've got
  twice as much junk).
+ Put a mirror on the bottom of the oven when
  cleaning it so you can see how well you're
  cleaning the top without having to bend.
+ Put an old shaving mirror on a wire handle so kids
  can **look around corners**.
+ **Increase light** around the house. Mirrors reflect
  light and make a room look bigger. Either hang
  mirrors as you would a picture, place them over
  tabletops, fit at the back of a shelf, put on the
  bottom of a wardrobe or fix along a fence line in
  the garden. You could also use a mirror along a
  fence line to reflect sun to a poorly lit clothesline.
+ If the mirror is old and the backing has worn off,

it's expensive to have it resilvered. Instead, use **glass paint and make a design** on the front of the mirror to cover the spotting. If the mirror is worn at the edges, glue lace fabric to each corner.

SAVE: *DRAWERS*

OTHER USES:

+ Use drawers as **storage** under the bed, in the attic, garage or under the house. They're easy to stack and you could add castors to the base to make moving them easier.
+ Turn two drawers into a storage **suitcase**. Sit one drawer, right side up, on a work surface and turn another one upside down and place it on top. Add two hinges to the back of the drawers and two catches either side of the drawer handle

TIP: To clean timber surfaces, combine 1 teaspoon of beeswax, 1 drop of lavender oil and 1 drop of lemon oil on a cloth. Warm in a microwave for 30 seconds or until it softens, allow to cool. You can use this on any timber surface.

TIP: Shannon places old perfume bottles at the back of drawers to scent clothes. You can leave them there for up to a year.

CHANGE FOR GOOD: The population of brown pelicans on the West Coast of the United States went into sharp decline from the 1940s to the 1970s mainly because of the use of the pesticide DDT. It was banned in the US in 1972, however it remains in the environment for a long time. Since the1980s brown pelican numbers have increased and as a result the US Fish and Wildlife Service has announced pelicans will be removed from the endangered species list.

SAVE: TISSUE BOXES

OTHER USES:

+ Keep **chalks and crayons** inside. They're easy to reach into, provide a lot of storage and are lightweight. And you can look through the clear plastic to see exactly what's inside.
+ The kids may want to decorate the boxes and **store small items**, such as Lego, in them.

Clothing and accessories

Buying clothes is expensive but there are many ways to get the most from your wardrobe. The most economical way to buy clothes, no matter what your age or gender, is to have items that coordinate and can be worn in different combinations so you get several looks from the same pieces. Stick to a consistent colour palette, choose durable classics and freshen up your look with cheaper seasonal items and accessories. At the beginning of spring and autumn, do a wardrobe audit. If you haven't worn something all season work out why. Are repairs needed? Are there stains? Is it uncomfortable? Do you dislike the fabric? Take a note of these things so the next time you go shopping you won't make the same mistakes. Either donate unwanted clothes to charity, sell them to a second-hand shop or recycle them (see suggestions under Old Clothes). Clothes can also be put into long-term storage if you think you might want to wear them in the future. It's good to work out what clothes you love and wear to death and why they appeal to you. If you have a checklist when selecting clothes, you'll end up with a wardrobe you love rather than having buyer's remorse.

Always buy the best quality you can afford. As a general rule, clothes made from natural fabrics last longer and are cheaper and easier to clean because they can be washed and stains float out of the fibres more readily. Synthetic fabrics hold stains and odours, need more frequent cleaning and often require dry-cleaning (which is expensive and not environmentally friendly).

You'll get more life from your clothes if you care for them properly. Do any mending before washing or the tear will get worse. When washing clothes, Shannon recommends using ½–⅔ less detergent than recommended on the packet. To work out if you're using too much, check if there are any bubbles at the end of the wash cycle. If there are, you're using too much detergent, which means excess soap gets into the fibres of clothes making them stiff and brittle. It also means the clothes will attract more dirt. Excessive bleaching puts pressure on the fibres and wears them down more quickly.

Protect your clothes and keep your wardrobe and drawers pest free. Combine 2 bay leaves (deters other varieties of insects including moths), 5 whole cloves (kills mould spores and deters silverfish), 1 tea bag (kills dust mites), 1–2 heads of lavender (adds fragrance and deters flying insects), 2 cedar chips (deters other varieties of insects including moths), 1 tablespoon of bicarb (absorbs moisture and helps prevent mould) in a bowl. Place the mixture in the centre of a small piece of muslin, cotton voile or pantyhose foot and tie up with string or ribbon.

TIP: To remove moisture from a wardrobe, tie 6–12 pieces of chalk together and hang them from the rail or a hook, avoiding direct contact with the clothes. The chalk absorbs moisture and can be dried out in the sun. Have two sets so you can rotate them. If moisture is a constant problem, you may need to add vents. If the rear wall of a built-in wardrobe is damp, add a false wall of cedar ply. Allow air to circulate behind a freestanding wardrobe. Don't position built-in wardrobes along exterior walls because you're more likely to get condensation.

Successful second-hand shopping

Look for good-quality fabric when choosing clothes at a second-hand store. If you don't want to do any mending, make sure the article fits well and check that the seams aren't worn, the zipper works and the buttons are intact. Don't worry about stains (unless they're really bad) because most can be removed. Second-hand clothes from charity stores tend to be cleaned well. However, if you're worried that they may not be, add 2 teaspoons of tea tree oil to a regular wash cycle or pour a kettle full of boiling water into the laundry tub or a bucket, add a couple of drops of tea tree oil, drop in the clothes (check the labels before you do this or you could damage the garments in the boiling water), drain them and drip-dry on the clothesline in the sunshine.

TIP: If you can't sew on buttons, use a button attacher.

SAVE: FUR COATS

OTHER USES:

+ If you've inherited an old fur coat, don't throw it away. It can become a luxurious **pillow or a throw** for the couch.
+ Convert it into a **fancy dress costume**.
+ Use as the covering for a **child's toy**.
+ Make your own **teddy bear**.

+ Use as cushioning on **backpack straps**.
+ Use to create a removable **collar and cuffs** for your favourite cardigan or jumper.
+ Turn into a **handbag, slippers or hat**.

SAVE: OLD CLOTHES

OTHER USES:

+ You should never find yourself throwing clothes in the bin unless it's a charity bin! **Charity bins and charity stores** are located all over the place and love receiving clean clothes.
+ Find out if anyone else wants your clothes. Organise a **clothes-swapping party** with similar-sized friends and exchange unwanted clothes.
+ Schools often like using old clothes for **craft projects**.
+ **Patchwork quilting** places love natural fabrics.
+ You can make some money at **recycling or vintage shops** that sell old clothes. You could also check out options online.
+ Get together with friends and have a **stall at the markets**.
+ Once you've exhausted all these options, remove the buttons and zips for your sewing kit and use the fabric as **cleaning rags** or as patches to repair other clothes.

TIP: Turn old jeans into a handbag—they already have a zipper and pocket. Cut off the legs 10 centimetres below the crotch and split the crotch seam. Turn the jeans inside out, lay them flat and run a seam across the bottom. Thread a belt through the belt loops as a handle or use fabric from the legs to make the strap.

SAVE: *T-SHIRTS*

OTHER USES:

+ Because T-shirts are **lint free** they make perfect cleaning cloths.

+ Wrap an old T-shirt over the end of a broom when

cleaning the floor instead of using a mop. You can wash the T-shirt and use it again and again.

+ If you've dropped something small on the ground, place an old T-shirt over the tube of a **vacuum cleaner** and secure with a rubber band. The vacuum cleaner will suck it up but it won't go into the barrel because the T-shirt will catch it.

SAVE: BUTTONS

OTHER USES:

+ Create a **button box**, if you don't have one already, to store excess buttons. If you have a button emergency you can usually find a good substitute for the missing button. Any container will do. Just make sure it's sturdy and big enough.
+ Use buttons to make **jewellery**. Use a hot glue gun to attach the buttons to fishing line to make necklaces and bracelets.
+ Use them to **decorate gift card**s.
+ Old buttons can be turned into **belts**. Simply line them up side by side or slightly overlap them so that they appear like fish scales along an existing belt. Use a hot glue gun to secure them.
+ Add them to the **busy box**.

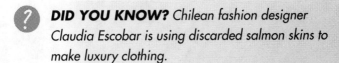

DID YOU KNOW? *Chilean fashion designer Claudia Escobar is using discarded salmon skins to make luxury clothing.*

SAVE: *TIES*

OTHER USES:

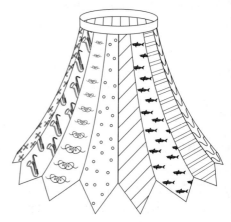

+ Turn old silk ties into a **skirt**. Undo the back seams, line them up side by side and sew them together. The fabric is great quality and it makes an interesting pattern.
+ Women can thread them through trousers as a decorative **belt**.
+ Turn a tie into a woman's **headscarf**.
+ Keep them for **patching** other clothes.
+ Add them to the **kids' dress-up box**.

SAVE: *SHIRTS*

OTHER USES:

+ Make a cover for a **cushion**.
+ Turn them into **work shirts** and use them when gardening. The pocket is particularly handy to store items in and the shirt protects your skin from the sun, keeps dirt off you and is lightweight.
+ Turn them into children's **smocks** to protect their clothes when painting or doing craft.
+ Save for **patchwork quilting** or the rag bag.

SAVE: UNDERPANTS

OTHER USES:

+ Remove the gusset and put cotton underpants in your **rag bag**.

+ Nylon knickers (minus the gusset) are great to use in the kitchen as **polishing cloths**.

SAVE: BRAS

OTHER USES:

+ As a child, Shannon used old bras to **catapult** fruit when playing with kids in the neighbourhood!

+ If your bra hook becomes squashed, **replace** it. Rather than just replacing the hook, it's easier to remove the elastic and the hooks from an old bra and attach it to the damaged bra.

+ Cut off the cups and use the elastic as an **occy strap** to wrap around items.

+ Use old bra cups to **protect Christmas decorations**, such as glass baubles.

SAVE: HANDBAGS

OTHER USES:

+ Use to store a **sewing kit**. Handbags are designed to carry lots of little items so they're perfect for storing needles, thread, zippers and other sewing bits and bobs.

+ Turn into a **jewellery case**.

+ Store precious **papers**. It's well insulated, easy to transport and can be stored anywhere.
+ Use as a **vase for flowers**. Line with plastic, put in an oasis block and arrange your flowers.

SAVE: SUNGLASSES

OTHER USES:

+ Keep in the hope that they'll come back into **fashion**.
+ Add to the **kids' dress-up box**.
+ Pop the lenses out, glue lace and glitter around the edge and make a **fairy mask**. Or glue some black felt or velvet around the edge to make a **Batman mask**.
+ Keep for **masquerades**.
+ Use the hinges on sunglasses to **repair jewellery**, such as catches for bracelets.

SAVE: SUNGLASSES CASES

OTHER USES:

+ They make great jewellery boxes.
+ Use to **store cosmetics**. This is particularly good when travelling.

SAVE: SCARVES

OTHER USES:

+ Cut into **smaller scarves** to wrap around ponytails.

+ Tear into strips and use to tie up fragile items in the **garden**.
+ Put in the **kids' dress-up box**.
+ Make into a **belt**.
+ Turn into a **cushion cove**r. Attach the scarf to some cotton backing so it won't pucker, sew onto an existing cushion cover or make a new one.

SAVE: *OLD KEYS*

OTHER USES:

+ Use as **curtain weight**s. Place them in the hem of curtains.
+ Put in the kids' busy box to make into **wind chimes**.

SAVE: *COSTUME JEWELLERY*

OTHER USES:

+ Use for **beading**, or adding bling to clothing.
+ Use for **Christmas decorations**.
+ Put in the **kids' dress-up box**.

SAVE: *BELTS*

OTHER USES:

+ Use them to **strap up suitcases or boxes**.
+ **Replace broken handles** on handbags and suitcases.
+ Keep a belt in the car in case you need to **tie something down**.
+ Use as a **tie on garden stakes**. You can easily undo them and tie them back up again.

SAVE: *GLOVES*

OTHER USES:

+ Cut off the fingers and make **mittens** to use in the garden.
+ Turn them into **finger puppets** and place in the kid's play box.
+ **Store jewellery** in them.
+ Fill with sawdust or sand, tie off the wrist and use as a quirky pincushion.

SAVE: *OLD SHOES*

OTHER USES:

+ If the shoes still have value, take them to a **charity or vintage shop** or sell them online.
+ Turn into **seedling boxes** or pot plants. They look very amusing placed under a tree.

 TIP: If you get tar on your shoes, remove it with baby oil.

DID YOU KNOW? *Before the advent of plastic, the leather from old shoes was often turned into washers to use in taps and cisterns.*

SAVE: *SHOE BOXES*

OTHER USES:

+ Keep your **receipts** in them for tax time.
+ Wrap them in colourful paper to create a **gift box**.

+ Use as a container for making **coconut ice**. Place
  boxes in the sunshine for a couple of hours to air
  and allow UV to kill any bacteria. The cardboard
  removes the excess moisture from the coconut
  ice to give a crisper edge and a lighter finish.
  When coconut ice is stored in a plastic or metal
  container it becomes a bit gummy and sticky.
  The cardboard is also easy to dispose of in the
  recycling bin.
+ Use for **storage**.

SAVE: SOCKS

OTHER USES:

+ Make a **soap sock**. If you have sensitive skin, put
  some soap inside a sock (so that you have soap
  and washer all in one) and use when showering:
  it's softer on your skin.
+ Use as **exfoliators** in the shower.
+ Place **over golf clubs** to protect them.
+ Turn into hand puppets and put in the **kids' play box**.
+ Use to **store coins**. Keep an old sock on a hook
  and when it's full, take it to the bank.
+ Use to **package** delicate gifts.
+ If your shoes are a bit smelly, make a **shoe frou**:
  combine 2 tablespoons of bicarb (absorbs odours
  and moisture), 2 tablespoons of talcum powder
  (absorbs moisture and gives a silky feel), 1 drop of

tea tree oil (kills tinea), 1 drop of oil of cloves (kills mould spores) and 1 drop of lavender oil (adds fragrance and deters insects) in a small bowl and mix well. Place the mixture in an old sock and tie with string or ribbon. Bounce the shoe frou in the offending shoes firmly. Reuse as needed.

+ Great for polishing when placed over your hands.

How to darn a sock

Use matching or contrasting cotton or wool and thread onto a needle. Make a running stitch around the hole to prevent it from fraying. Place a darning egg—if you don't have one use a boiled egg or an incandescent light bulb—in the sock so that you have a curved edge to follow. Start from one side of the hole, weave to the other side, pick up a woven stitch and weave back to the other side of the hole. Do this in both directions until the hole is completely covered. To finish off, weave the thread away from the hole for around 2 centimetres and cut.

SAVE: *PANTYHOSE*

OTHER USES:

+ Even if pantyhose are covered in ladders, never throw an old pair in the bin—they are a versatile item. The weave of pantyhose is based on silk and is very tough. When wet, the open rope mesh of fibres stick together to form a hard cord which is so strong, you can even **tow a car** with them.

+ Use as a **scourer** when cleaning teflon frying pans. Roll pantyhose into a ball and wipe over the pan. If the pan is very dirty, add bicarb and white vinegar.

+ Use to **polish saucepans**.

+ Keep to **clean taps**. Wrap pantyhose behind taps and use a seesaw action.

+ Use them to **clean the fridge**.

+ **Remove fingermarks and smears** from stainless steel (especially fridges) with a damp pair of pantyhose and then wipe over with a dry pair.

+ **Remove soap scum** with damp pantyhose.

+ **Clean ceilings**. Place pantyhose over a broom head, sprinkle lemon oil over the top and gently wipe along the ceiling. This removes dirt and webs and keeps spiders away.

+ **Clean ceiling fan blades**. Wipe the blades with damp pantyhose on a broom.

+ **Polish chrome furniture** to keep rusty spots at bay.

+ **Wipe highchairs** with damp pantyhose.

+ **Clean upholstery**. Combine unprocessed wheat bran and white vinegar until the mixture looks like brown sugar, place in the toe of a pair of pantyhose and use it like an eraser.

+ Use them to **clean the drum of washing machines and dryers**. Wipe over the tops and sides of the machines to clean.

+ Use them to **remove excess lint from the dryer**. Wipe over the drum, the edges of the lint catcher and anywhere else the lint gets stuck.
+ Put salt inside the pantyhose toe and **clean the tiles at the edge of the pool**.
+ Thread the legs of pantyhose through the arms of **jumpers** when drying on the clothesline. Peg the toes to the clothesline. This helps retain the shape and prevent peg marks.
+ **Protect delicate items** (such as lingerie and sequinned clothes) in the washing machine by placing them inside the legs of a pair of pantyhose, tie them off and place in the machine.
+ Use them to **store onions in the pantry**. Allow the pantyhose to hang so that air can circulate around the onions.
+ Use them for **tying and staking tomato plants**. It won't bruise the stems. They're handy to use when tying off grafts because they hold the graft firmly in place without crushing.
+ **Protect stone fruits and figs from birds** by putting the fruit into pantyhose. Birds don't like the feel of pantyhose in their beaks. This also keeps fruit fly away.
+ **Grow alfalfa** in a section of pantyhose about the size of a tennis ball. Mix equal parts sawdust and alfalfa seeds and put them inside the pantyhose and tie off tightly. Sit it on a saucer on a

windowsill, water regularly and trim the sprouts. There's no need for dirt.

+ Use pantyhose to tie and **hold tree branches in place**. This is perfect for citrus trees.

+ Use them as **hanging pots**. Pack the bottom of a leg with soil, add seeds and hang up (it will look like a sausage until the plants grow). This will only work with small-stemmed plants, such as maiden hair ferns or pansies.

+ **Clean pet bowls** by wiping over them with damp pantyhose. Wash the pantyhose before using them again.

+ Use them to make **fairy wings** for children. Take 2 coat-hangers, twist the hooks together, form the body of the coat-hanger into wing shapes and stretch pantyhose over each side. Tie off tightly at the centre and decorate with spray paint and glitter. Add tinsel along the edges of the wings.

+ Use old pantyhose to make **Halloween decorations**. Trim the elastic off the top and secure the waistband tightly over a doorframe with thumbtacks. Spread the legs around the frame. Use a hot knife or lit cigarette to burn holes in the pantyhose so that it looks like cobwebs. Don't use a candle or any flame.

+ Turn a coat-hanger into a loop and wrap the waistband of a pair of pantyhose around it to form a two-legged **yabby net**. Hold the hook of the coat-hanger in your hand and position it over a running current to collect yabbies for bait.

+ Use them to **wash the car**. Combine 1 cup of black tea and 1 cup of white vinegar in a bucket of water. If there are resin stains on your car, add 1 teaspoon of tea tree oil to the mixture. Place pantyhose over the head of a broom, dip into the bucket and sweep over the car. Throw the excess water over the car and rinse with a bucket of clean water. Use dry pair of pantyhose to polish windows and car edging.

+ If you have patterned pantyhose, cut a section from the legs and turn them into **mittens for children**, just like Madonna in the 1980s. Patterend pantyhose also make great gift bags, shoe frou holders and wardrobe sachets.

SAVE: YOGA MATS

OTHER USES:

+ Use as **lining in the boot of your car**.
+ Cut it to size and use in the **bathroom** under a bathmat for grip.
+ Use as a **camping mat**.

 DID YOU KNOW? *Many yoga mats contain PVC which isn't a sustainable resource. Newer eco ones are coming onto the market.*

Bathroom

The next time you're rinsing shampoo from your hair, take a look at the plug hole. See all those suds? We can almost guarantee you've created more than you need, so really those suds are money down the drain. More is not necessarily better when using most products in the bathroom! You don't need centimetres of toothpaste on your toothbrush or a bubbly lathering of soap. Think about cutting back just a little and see what a difference it makes. Even small changes will help you save money and time, and help the environment at the same time.

Also consider what other changes you can make to your bathroom. If your bathroom is dark, put in a skylight so you don't always have to turn on a light, or add extra mirrors or mirror tiles. Keep the room well ventilated to prevent mould and mildew from forming. If you haven't done so already, install water-efficient showerheads and dual-flush toilets to reduce water use.

SAVE FEATURE: It's so disappointing when your favourite lipsticks get low and you can't use the stubs that are left. Turn these stubs into lip gloss. Line a bowl with plastic wrap and use a lip brush to remove the last parts of the lipstick. Combine with equal parts lip balm and beeswax (available from the chemist or hardware store). Warm the mixture in a microwave in short bursts until it just melts. While still warm, roll into a sausage shape so it will fit into the old lipstick holder and place in the freezer until firm. Run the holder under hot water and then wedge the new lip gloss into it. The warmed holder will slightly melt the lip gloss so it sticks in place.

Shower/bath

According to the Australian Bureau of Statistics, in 2007 36.9 per cent of households saved water by showering less often or by taking shorter showers. Assist your water-saving ways by changing the showerhead. An average one uses about 15–25 litres of water per minute whereas a water efficient one uses 6–7 litres of water per minute because it has fewer and finer nozzles. To work out which showerhead is most efficient, consult the label. The best is a 3-star/AAA rating. Rather than heading to the shops, check out your water utility because it has many available at discounted prices.

 DID YOU KNOW? *The further your hot-water system is from the bathroom, the longer it takes to heat the water. If possible, locate the hot-water system near where it is used (including the kitchen and laundry). Insulate both hot and cold water pipes to reduce heat loss.*

TIP: If you've bought proprietary cleaning products, don't throw them out. There could be another use for them. For example, most cleaning products contain chlorine which can be used to clean the driveway (put ½ cup in a bucket of water and use a stiff broom). You can also use the same mixture on any hard outside surface (but not near plants) because chlorine dissipates in sunlight.

SAVE: SOAP

OTHER USES:

+ Place soap remnants in a jar, add water, shake vigorously and create your own **liquid soap**. It's a great cleaning agent for hard surfaces. For very dirty surfaces, try Shannon's toxic cleaner (it's not really toxic, it's just strong). Mix ½ cup of grated soap, 2 tablespoons of methylated spirits, ½ cup of vinegar and 2 tablespoons of bicarb. Seal the jar and shake it until all the ingredients are dissolved. Be warned: it's very strong and could eat into surfaces so do a test first.
+ Use old soap **to lubricate hinges and drawers**.

How to make your own bubble bath

Mix 120 ml of glycerine, 1 small bottle of cheap dishwashing liquid and 5–10 ml of your favourite essential oil, dilute by half and store in a clean, recycled bottle.

DID YOU KNOW? *A running tap releases around 9 litres of water a minute.*

TIP: In desperate times, save water by bathing Japanese-style—it's common for all household members to use the same water! First, soap your body and rinse with water using a washbowl then get into a hot bath and have a good soak.

TIP: Never use undiluted white vinegar on grout because the acid can eat into the porous surface. To make it usable, mix the white vinegar with bicarb or water. Mixing bicarb and vinegar creates a salt.

SAVE: SHOWER CURTAINS

OTHER USES:

+ Unless they're completely dirty, turn them into a **rain poncho**. Fold the curtain into quarters and cut out a hole for the head.
+ Use as a **drop sheet** when painting.
+ Use as a **play mat** when the kids are painting or playing with playdough.
+ Use as a **table protector**.

DID YOU KNOW? *Actor Jennifer Aniston says she's doing her bit for the environment by brushing her teeth in the shower. She says she cleans her teeth and body at the same time to save water and electricity. 'I take a three-minute shower. I even brush-wash-brush my teeth while I shower. Every two minutes in the shower uses as much water as a person in Africa uses for everything in their life for a whole day.'*

SAVE: METAL AND PLASTIC SHOWER CURTAIN RINGS

OTHER USES:

+ Keep **excess rings** in case one breaks.
+ Use as **key rings**.
+ Thread **dolly bits**, such as jewellery, on them.
+ Store **hair scrunchies** on them.

TIP: Give your bathroom a new look by making and installing a new shower curtain. For instructions, see *How to be Comfy*.

TIP: Keep a bucket in the shower to catch water before it gets hot. Use the water in the garden or washing machine, when rinsing the dishes or flushing the toilet.

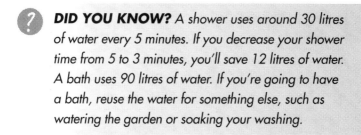

DID YOU KNOW? *A shower uses around 30 litres of water every 5 minutes. If you decrease your shower time from 5 to 3 minutes, you'll save 12 litres of water. A bath uses 90 litres of water. If you're going to have a bath, reuse the water for something else, such as watering the garden or soaking your washing.*

TIP: Keep an eye on how long you shower with a timer.

SAVE: SHOWER CAPS
OTHER USES:

+ Use them to **cover** the tops of stools. This means you can change the colour scheme really simply and they are easy to wipe or wash clean.

DID YOU KNOW? *People used to cover opened tins, jars and pudding bowls with old shower caps because aluminium foil was so expensive.*

TIP: It's best not to use harsh chemicals and scourers to clean the bath or shower because they slowly wear away the surface and make it easier for dirt and bacteria to get trapped. If you have mould, add a couple of drops of oil of cloves to your wash water and apply with a cloth.

Is greywater safe?

Greywater is the water that goes down the drain when you bath, shower, wash your hands and do the laundry. Kitchen waste is generally not included in greywater nor is toilet waste, which is known as blackwater. Some households produce up to 400 litres of greywater a day, which can be diverted to the garden or stored in a tank. You can also install a greywater system in the bathroom to flush the toilet. There are several ways to capture and reuse this water and many experts believe the simpler (and cheaper) diversion systems work the best. Be aware that care needs to be taken when using greywater because it can contain bacteria. Regulations vary from state to state but generally you can't allow greywater to run off into stormwater drains. It's best not to use this water on vegie patches but it's fine to use on fruit trees. Don't overwater or allow water to pool because bacteria and insect larvae breed in still water. Always be mindful what you put down the drain!

TIP: Fix dripping taps. All that wasted water adds up!

TIP: If your drains smell, it could be from a build-up of talcum powder or other foreign material. To fix the smell, put ½ cup of bicarb down the drain, then add ½ cup of white vinegar. Leave for half an hour then pour boiling water down the drain. To

stop the problem recurring, keep talcum powder (and foreign material) away from the drain.

Before calling a plumber, see if you can fix a problem yourself and save some money. One common bathroom problem is a blocked S-bend. As we discussed in *How to be Comfy*, place a bucket underneath the S-bend to capture any water and gunk. Wear rubber gloves for grip, and unscrew the two big nuts located either side of the S-bend. PVC pipes can usually be removed with your hands. Metal pipes will need a monkey grip, Stillson or large adjusting spanner. After releasing the 'S', clean it out by flushing with water. Make sure you use a different tap (or bucket) or you'll flood the bathroom. If there's gunk in the fixed part of the pipes, refashion a coat-hanger into a loop and attach a scourer (cut to size) to the end with string. Work it up and down the pipes to clean out the gunk. Replace the 'S', making sure it's secure or water will leak. Put 1 tablespoon of bicarb down the sink, followed by 1 tablespoon of white vinegar. Leave for 10 minutes then flush hot water down the pipes. Proprietary products are available to clear pipes but they're incredibly toxic, damaging to the environment and can burn your skin, so always wear gloves and goggles and take care. If the sink is really blocked, you may need to get a plumber.

SAVE: BATHMATS

OTHER USES:

+ Use them to sit on when **gardening**.
+ Keep them at the edge of the swimming pool to **dry damp feet**.
+ Put them at the front door when it's raining for **muddy shoes**.
+ Use as **bedding for a pet**. If they're waterproof, put across pet cages when it's raining.

SAVE: SHAMPOO, CONDITIONER AND MOUTHWASH BOTTLES

OTHER USES:

+ Clean out the bottles with dishwashing liquid and hot water and rinse with a small amount of white vinegar and water. Use them to **store liquids**, such as laundry detergent, when travelling.
+ Put the tail ends of all your shampoo bottles into one bottle and store in the **laundry**. Do the same with hair conditioner. It's great for washing woollens.
+ Create a **tenpin bowling** set (see page 210).

DID YOU KNOW? *Shannon has found that doing two washes with a small amount of shampoo is better at removing sweat and oils from your hair than one larger wash. The reason is shampoo emulsifies oil in your hair and helps it rinse out more easily.*

How to make your own hair treatment

Beat 3 eggs, add 2 tablespoons of olive oil and 1 teaspoon of lemon juice or, if your hair is dry, orange juice. Apply the mixture to your hair and cover with plastic wrap. Leave for 30 minutes, wash out, shampoo and condition. To give your hair a really shiny look, wash in shampoo, rinse then wash in 600 ml of beer. Leave for 30 minutes, rinse in clean water, dry and style as usual. You'll have a mirror sheen!

TIP: If you have hair that tangles easily, place 2 teaspoons of cheap hair conditioner into a 1-litre spray bottle of water and mist it over your hair. It's much cheaper than proprietary options and is just as good!

DID YOU KNOW? *If you have long hair and decide to cut it short, you can sell it to wig makers, as Jennifer's sister did. They could also become hair extensions.*

WHY IT MATTERS: Research from the University of London has linked the onset of male pattern baldness to environmental factors such as air pollution and smoking. While baldness is hereditary, men living in polluted areas are more likely to go bald than those in cleaner environments.

SAVE: TOWELS

OTHER USES:

+ Turn them into **face washers**. You can make six from a small towel or eight from a large towel.
+ Rip them into smaller squares and use them as **rags to clean the floor**. They're excellent for polishing.
+ If you have a swimming pool, **store** old towels near the back door so people can dry themselves before heading into the house.
+ Use for **packing and wrapping**.
+ **Freshen up** by dyeing a new colour.
+ Turn them into **bar towels**.
+ Keep to **mop up spills**.
+ Make your own **shower robe**.
+ If **transporting food**, wrap it in old towels and place in a basket. It'll stay warm.

TIP: You can buy towelling by the metre and make your own towels using iron-on hem binding. Decorate them and give them as gifts.

Hot-water systems

A quarter of the average household energy bill comes from heating water. If you're buying a new system there are a few types to choose from. Storage tanks powered by electricity or gas hold litres of warmed water ready for use. Another system is instantaneous hot water that heats water as it is needed. When you turn on the tap, cold water travels through the water pipe into the unit and an element heats the water. It can be powered by electricity or gas with gas being more energy efficient. Instantaneous gas water heaters save emissions by heating only the water you need. You can also have a solar hot-water system with gas or electric boosters in case there isn't enough sun. A gas-boosted solar hot-water system is the most greenhouse friendly way to heat your water. The upfront cost is higher but you'll save over the years. Do your homework first.

DID YOU KNOW? *Reducing the temperature on your hot-water thermostat by 5°C can reduce your water heating bill by up to 20 per cent.*

TIP: If you're going away on holiday, save money by turning the hot-water system off. You'll save power because you won't heat water that isn't used. See if you can find a neighbour or friend to turn it back on for you a day before you get back so the water is hot.

Vanity

The next time you're washing your hands and you squirt liquid soap from a pump pack, notice how much you use. Do you really need that amount to wash your hands? The manufacturer thinks so. The more you use, the more you'll need to buy. Our suggestions are to press only halfway or add water to the mixture in the container. You could also put a piece of sticky tape around the tubing under the nozzle to reduce how much the pump can press and dispense.

SAVE: SOAP DISPENSERS
OTHER USES:

+ The most obvious thing to do with a dispenser is to **refill and reuse** it. They're handy in the kitchen for storing dishwashing liquid and have the added advantage of dispensing a metered dose.
+ Sterilise and **store food** in them. To sterilise, combine 1 tablespoon of white vinegar, 2 teaspoons of uncooked rice and a dash of bicarb and place in the dispenser. Shake and rinse in boiling water,

making sure you thoroughly clean the pump pack
tube in boiling water as well. Refill the packs with
maple syrup, honey (but not if you store it in the
fridge because the honey will go too hard for the
pump action to work), ice-cream toppings and
smooth jam. They're also great for storing tomato
sauce and one squirt is the perfect amount for a
sandwich. The seal in the dispenser blocks the
entry of ants so once it has been filled it can be
stored in the cupboard.

+ Store **lotions, potions, shampoos and conditioners**
in them. Because it dispenses a metered dose, it's
perfect people who overuse products.

TIP: If you can, avoid having items made of metal in the
bathroom because they may leave rust marks. This is
particularly the case with aerosol cans. If you have
cans in the bathroom, seal the base by applying clear
nail polish to stop them from rusting.

SAVE: COMBS

OTHER USES:

+ Use to **store fuse wire**. Wrap the wire through the
teeth of the comb.

+ **Store ribbon**. Wrap the ribbon end to end
lengthways and then wind the last bit through the
teeth. Doing this means you don't have to fix the

end with a pin, which can leave rust marks.

+ If you get a pull in a jumper, use a wide-tooth comb on either side of the pull to **stretch the fibres** evenly back into place.

+ When putting fine-grade seeds in a potting tray, **comb the seeds** into the top of the soil.

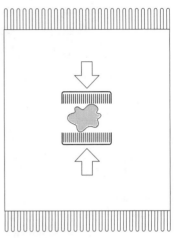

+ Keep combs in your cleaning kit to **pick up messy items** from carpet. Slide the combs together to lift, rather than squash, the debris.

+ Use in the **kids' sandbox** as a road grader.

SAVE: TOOTHBRUSHES

OTHER USES:

+ Toothbrushes are perfect for cleaning anything that's small. Use them to clean under **taps** and for attacking **grout**.

+ Use toothbrushes to remove **stains** from carpet. Make sure you rub the carpet fibre in all four directions when removing a stain.

+ Use as a miniature **nail brush**.

+ The fine bristles make an excellent **jewellery cleaner**.

+ They're easy for children to hold, so use them when **splatter painting**. To splatter paint, place a piece of flyscreen above a sheet of paper, dip the old toothbrush in children's paint and run the brush across the screen to create patterns.
+ Clean the inside **necks of jugs and vases**.
+ Temporarily stop a **banging cupboard door**! Cut a toothbrush handle off with a utility knife and fix the back of the head with double-sided tape to the inside of the cupboard. The cupboard door will hit the bristles.
+ Attach to a bench in the workshop to **clean files and other tools**. A toothbrush is great for removing metal filings and cleaning saw edges.
+ Use to **polish small straps** on shoes.
+ A toothbrush is ideal as a **brush for dolls' hair**.
+ When using **chalk on a blackboard**, stop the squeaking noise by rubbing a toothbrush over the chalk to dull the surface.

SAVE: TOOTHPASTE CONTAINERS AND REMNANTS

OTHER USES:

+ Don't throw out a used-toothpaste container. It can be used like a big marker. Cut off the tail end and use the empty tube to **store poster paint**. Seal with a bulldog clip.
+ Keep toothpaste remnants for **stain removal**.

Toothpaste contains bicarb and silicone particles making it a great abrasive. To make an instant cream cleanser, fill ⅓ of the tube with water, screw on the lid and shake. Use for rust spots on vanities.

+ As a temporary measure, paint toothpaste across the edges of smooth tiles and allow it to dry. It makes them **non-skid**.

+ Add old toothpaste to kid's paint to provide profile or thickness and give an embossed look and peppermint perfume. This is perfect for decorating **gift cards**.

Can toothpaste clear up pimples?

The topic of how to get rid of zits is always popular in the school playground. The toothpaste solution has been mooted for years and whether it works depends on the type of toothpaste and your skin. If it has lots of baking soda in it, it can alleviate the symptoms. At the same time, putting a dab of toothpaste on broken skin could lead to further breakouts because some toothpaste contains sugar! Shannon recommends applying diluted tea tree oil and no squeezing.

DID YOU KNOW? *In 2007, 23.9 per cent of Australians saved water by turning the tap off while cleaning their teeth. Cleaning your teeth with the tap running uses 9 litres of water each minute. Turned off, you use 1 litre of water each minute. Don't wet your toothbrush before applying toothpaste because you dilute the effectiveness of your toothpaste and it wastes water.*

SAVE: DENTAL FLOSS

OTHER USES:

+ Dental floss is made of nylon or cotton with a wax coating and is incredibly strong. If you get a burr on jewellery, you can **file** it off with dental floss.
+ Use as **thread** for sewing on buttons or any other kind of mending.
+ Use as **hair ties** on braids (but not with used dental floss!). This is easier than chunky elastic bands.

SAVE: DENTAL FLOSS CONTAINERS

OTHER USES:

+ Use to **store embroidery yarn** or any fibre small enough to come through the hole, such as fuse wire. It'll have a minty smell as well.
+ Store items such as **staples and paper clips** in them in your study.

DID YOU KNOW? *Shannon uses old tablet blister packs when painting. It means she can cover the paint with the foil flap when she's making a cup of tea!*

WHY IT MATTERS: In unseasonably warm weather in 2005 there were more people with chest pains visiting NSW hospital emergency departments. Researchers believe the chest pains were linked to high solar radiance and ozone levels.

SAVE: RAZOR BLADES

OTHER USES:

+ Remember when you needed a razor blade to remove the old registration sticker from the windscreen of your car? There's no need to save them for that purpose any more but they come in handy for other jobs such as **removing pilling** (those annoying little balls) from jumpers or flannelette sheets. Simply shave over the affected areas. Keep one next to the iron ready for action.

+ **Clean paint specks** off glass. Just be careful of fingers.

TIP: One way to make razors last longer is to coat the blade in olive oil so it doesn't rust. Just make sure you remove the olive oil film with warm water before shaving or you might nick yourself.

Rust can also be prevented if you keep razors in a dry environment, such as the freezer. Shannon keeps a small tray in the edge of her freezer for steel wool and razor blades.

TIP: When shaving, run a little water into a plugged sink or use a shaving mug. Rinsing a razor blade under a running tap wastes water.

SAVE: *FOUNDATION BOTTLES*

OTHER USES:

+ Many foundations come in pump packs. **Refill** and use them to carry hand lotion or any other kind of lotion. They're a perfect size for the handbag or glove box.
+ **Reuse** the old bottles in the kitchen or laundry.

SAVE: *PERFUME BOTTLES*

OTHER USES:

+ **Refills** can be purchased for some perfumes, which cuts back on the amount of packaging used.
+ Fill perfume bottles with water and use as a **face spritz**.
+ Use refillable bottles to store **homemade insecticide** to tackle garden nasties. For a general pest deterrent, simmer 1 chopped onion, 1 clove of garlic and 1 tablespoon of cayenne pepper in

2 litres of water. Allow the mixture to stand for
1 month. Mix 1 tablespoon of the mixture with
1 litre of water and spray over the garden.

+ Combine **SPF 30+ sunscreen** with water, place it
  in an old perfume bottle and spray it over your
  body.

+ Make your own **toilet spray**. Combine 1 teaspoon
  of lavender oil with 2 cups of water and pour into
  a refillable spray bottle. Spray into the bowl to
  create a non-stick surface.

> **?** **DID YOU KNOW?** *Arum lily bulbs can be turned
> into a face mask. Grind the bulb and place on paper
> towel until it dries out. Then mix with a small amount of
> water and apply as a face mask. Leave for 10 minutes.
> It's great for zits and bleaching freckles!*

SAVE: *EYE SHADOW/BLUSHER*

OTHER USES:

+ Put remnants in the **children's paintbox**. It's perfect
  for painting on tissue paper and when painting
  pastel sky scenes.

+ Use to reapply **dolls' make-up**.

SAVE: MAKE-UP BRUSHES

OTHER USES:

+ Use to **clean** around small pieces of machinery.
+ **Dust** delicate china ornaments with them.
+ Mascara brushes are great for **accessing tiny places**. Shannon uses the applicator for fluxing when soldering. Clean the mascara brush and bottle with methylated spirits and then wash in dishwashing liquid and water. Store in a jar ready for any use.

TIP: To get out the last skerrick of mascara, stand the tube in a glass of hot water. If it's dried out, hold mascara with a pair of tongs to protect your fingers from the hot steam and place the mouth over a boiling kettle.

SAVE: HAIR DRYER

OTHER USES:

+ Use to **remove dust** from artificial or dried flowers. It also removes dust from porcelain.
+ Use to remove **spilt wax**. Place paper towel over the spill and aim the hair dryer over the stain. The wax will melt and become absorbed into the paper towel.
+ **Speed up** the drying process. Use on damp mattresses or clothes.
+ Shannon uses a hairdryer when **painting water colours** to dry them quickly.

Toilet

We can all be thankful that sanitation has come a long way in the last 50 years. Before then, many cities and towns didn't have a sewerage system and a so-called 'dunny man' would drive his truck in the little lane behind houses collecting toilet pans. You can just imagine the stench! These days, there are waste management conventions (as showcased in the film *Kenny*). The other big change with toilets is the amount of water needed to flush them. Older toilets use about 18 litres of water per flush. Newer ones use 6 litres for a full flush or 3 litres for a half flush, which is a huge difference. Toilets are easy to convert to dual flush. Buy the appropriate self-contained mechanism to go inside the cistern or do what they did years ago and put a brick in the cistern.

SAVE: TOILET PAPER ROLLS

OTHER USES:

+ Old toilet paper rolls can be very handy around the home. Help your children organise their drawers and **place socks or undies in them**. They're easy to see and the drawers will look more organised.

+ Toilet rolls can be used to **store posters**. For longer posters, stack the toilet rolls one on top of the other.

+ Local preschools often use toilet rolls for **craft**, so ask if they'd like your excess ones.

+ If giving jewellery as a gift, **giftwrap** it using a toilet roll. Place the jewellery inside an old toilet roll, pinch either end to keep the jewellery secure and wrap it up.

+ Use to dispose of sanitary supplies or sharps.

TIP: Cut back on toilet paper use by slightly squashing the roll so it doesn't turn as easily on the roll holder. This is particularly helpful if you have young children in your house.

DID YOU KNOW? *Toilet paper made from recycled paper has been around for years but some people complain that it's a bit scratchy. Perhaps this information will assist you in your choice: non-recycled paper is soft and white because it usually comes from virgin wood pulp that is often bleached. According to Planet Ark, the average Australian household uses 94 rolls of toilet paper every year. If each household substituted four rolls of ordinary toilet tissue with recycled toilet tissue, an extra 10,000 tonnes of office paper could be recycled.*

TIP: Make your own air freshener for the toilet: it's cheaper, smells nicer and there's no empty can to throw away. To do this, fill a spray pack with water and add your favourite essential oil. Lavender, mint or thyme oil are all good choices. If you like a fresh, pine smell in your bathroom, place some diosma, which releases a piney fragrance, in a vase on the vanity or cistern.

DID YOU KNOW? *According to the Australian Bureau of Statistics, 81.3 per cent of West Australian households have dual-flush toilets in their homes—this is the greatest proportion in Australia.*

TIP: Don't keep old toilet brushes because they're unhygienic.

How to stop water leaking inside the cistern

You'll waste valuable water if you have a leak in your toilet. As we wrote in *How to be Comfy*, to fix a leak, remove the top of the cistern to look inside. Don't worry about any gunge—the water here is clean! Your cistern will contain either a ball float hanging from an inlet valve or have a self-contained mechanism, which is difficult to see inside. Some newer toilets have the cistern built into the wall and are harder to access. If you can see a ball float in your cistern, and the water is leaking,

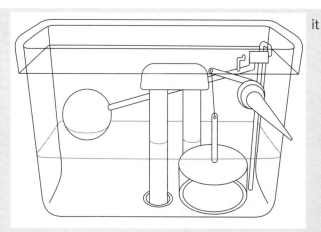

it

could be a problem with the valve mechanism or there could be a perished washer. To check, lift the float and if water stops running, you need to replace the ball valve mechanism. If water is released from the inlet valve, the washer may have perished. Washers are relatively cheap and easy to replace.

Another way to test if your cistern is leaking is to put in a little food colouring. If coloured water flows into the bowl without being flushed, you have a leak and the washer or ball valve washer needs to be replaced. There are many different washers available these days. Hardware stores have a rack of fix-a-tap cards with guide notes.

If you decide to replace the washer, be sure to turn the water off at the stop tap, usually located on the wall at the base of the toilet. Remove the pivot pin and undo the top of the inlet valve until you reach the sealing washer. Turn the washer over or replace it. If it's still leaking, you may have to replace the entire valve.

Should you let the yellow mellow?

In these water-aware times, many households apply the mantra 'if it's yellow, let it mellow'. This principle is fine but don't let urine sit in a toilet bowl for more than 12 hours because it will begin to eat into the porcelain. You can neutralise the acidity by adding 1 teaspoon of bicarb per wee.

 DID YOU KNOW? *According to the Australian Bureau of Statistics, in 1994 only 21.8 per cent of Australian households had a water efficient showerhead and 39 per cent had a dual-flush toilet. In 2007, 55.1 per cent of homes had water efficient showerheads and 80.9 per cent had dual-flush toilets.*

Kids

Children's growth spurts invariably cause money to leave your wallet at a furious rate! But there are tricks to help you extend the life of clothes and shoes and just about everything else that kids use. Why not make your own games and entertain children the old-fashioned way? And as for furniture and toys the kids have outgrown, most can be handed on to other family members or friends and some can be converted for other uses. And there's always the option of holding a garage sale!

It's a good idea to talk to your children about the environment and the little things they can do to make a big difference. Discuss the concept of recycling and why it's important to turn the light out when they're not in a room. Show them how to separate paper, metals and plastics and you'll be setting them up with good environmental habits for life. They'll probably start teaching you a thing or two.

SAVE FEATURE: Your daughter may not fit into her ballet tutu any more but don't throw it away: the tulle can be turned into a body sponge for the bathroom. Cut 1 metre of tulle 20 centimetres wide and fold it back and forth 10 times so that it resembles a fan. Make a running stitch down the middle of the folds and tie along the centre with rope, ribbon or whatever's handy to create a pompom. Hang it from a tap in the shower or bath. If you don't want to make a tulle pompom, you can resell tutus through dance schools.

Furnishing

It's easy to get carried away and buy too much stuff when you're having your first child. One thing to remember is to go for practicality over looks. Jennifer's friends had a top-of-the-line highchair that was too cumbersome to adjust and they ended up using one bought at a garage sale for $20.

Some companies produce furniture that can be converted as your child grows: cots become beds and chairs, change tables become desks, and highchairs turn into chairs.

It's very common for people to pass on used children's furniture and most is in perfectly good condition. One important point to check is compliance with the mandatory standard. To see if there have been recalls, visit www.accc.gov.au and look under current safety alerts. The site also includes the helpful publication *Keeping Baby Safe: A guide to nursery furniture.*

Make some money by selling no-longer-needed children's furniture online—you might be surprised by how much you can make. If it's too worn, consider these other uses.

SAVE: COTS

OTHER USES:

+ Use a cot as storage for **pool toys**. Because it has slats, water will drain away easily.
+ Remove the sliding panel, paint the cot in bright colours and keep **stuffed toys** inside. It's like a huge basket off the floor.
+ If damaged, pull it apart and put the timber in

your **lumber pile** for other building projects.
+ Remove the panels and use as trellises for growing
  vines and sweet peas in the garden.

> **TIP:** Used baby mattresses can now be professionally
> cleaned and disinfected. You can also pass on tea
> tree mattresses but handwash them first. Dry
> them on top of the clothesline, flipping them
> regularly.

SAVE: *BABY MANCHESTER*

OTHER USES:
+ The filling used in pillows is breathable and washable,
  so it can be turned into **stuffing for toys or cushions**.
+ Use old sheets to **cover food** to keep flies and
  mozzies away when entertaining outside. They're
  a good size, lightweight and washable.
+ Make **patchwork quilts** from old sheets,
  pillowcases, doona covers and blankets.

SAVE: *HIGHCHAIRS*

OTHER USES:
+ A highchair past its use-by date can be turned into
  a **pot stand**.
+ Bracket shelves inside the legs to create storage.
  Use to **store pots and pans** in the kitchen.

TIP: Always clean highchairs after each meal because once food sets, it's harder to remove. If you miss a bit and it's now like cement, wring a sponge in hot water and place it over the hardened food. Leave for 10 minutes. Then wipe over the area with a couple of drops of tea tree oil on a clean damp cloth.

TIP: Tea tree oil is a great non-toxic steriliser. Add 1 teaspoon to 1 litre of water in a spray pack to clean hard furnishings and hard toys.

SAVE: PRAMS

OTHER USES:

+ Shannon loves Victorian wicker prams particularly because of the suspension. Modern prams are made of aluminium, steel or chrome which can be **recycled**. Aluminium ones can be worth a bit of money (think about how many soft drink cans it would equal). Find your nearest scrap metal recycler in the Yellow Pages.

+ An old pram is great to **stack newspapers for delivery** if your child has a paper run.

+ Shannon uses an old pram to **cart potting mix** in the garden.

TIP: They're less common these days but if you have an old bassinet, use it to store rolled-up towels and linen. It can easily be stored under a table or on a shelf. You could also use it to store firewood or magazines. And you could spray paint it to match the room.

SAVE: BUNNY RUGS

OTHER USES:

+ Turn into **patchwork cuddle blankets**. Remove damaged areas from two or four bunny rugs, cut the remnants into the desired shape and stitch together. They're lightweight and easy to store. You can change the colour by dyeing them.

+ Turn bunny rugs into a **child's kimono-style dressing gown**. They're easy to wash and the fabric is soft but tough wearing. Lay an old bunny rug out flat and fold the two outside edges into the middle (this forms  the centre front). Measure your child around the hips and allow 1 centimetre for the seam on either side. Cut the excess material from either side of

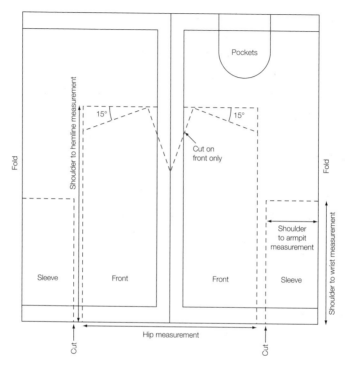

Fold

Shoulder to hemline measurement

15°

Pockets

15°

Cut on
front only

Fold

Shoulder
to armpit
measurement

Shoulder to wrist measurement

Sleeve

Front

Front

Sleeve

Cut

Hip measurement

Cut

the bunny rug—this will become the fabric for the
sleeves. Measure from the bottom edge of the rug
for the shoulder height and cut the shoulder on a
15° angle towards the neck (see diagram). Then
cut the centre front trim in a V shape to the
shoulder line from centre breast bone upwards.
Stitch the shoulder seams together. Cut the sleeves
to the appropriate length, keeping the bound
edge as the cuff. Set the sleeve into the shoulder

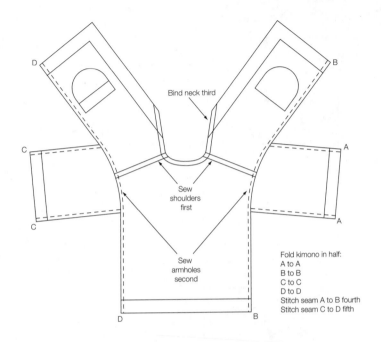

Bind neck third

Sew
shoulders
first

Sew
armholes
second

Fold kimono in half:
A to A
B to B
C to C
D to D
Stitch seam A to B fourth
Stitch seam C to D fifth

seam and stitch the side seams all the way from
the cuff to the bottom of the garment. Take an extra
bit of binding (use leftovers or new binding) for
the neckline. If sewing by hand, use wool thread
rather than cotton thread because it's softer and
grips the fabric better so you need fewer stitches.

SAVE: *CHANGE TABLE*

OTHER USES:

+ Use as a **sewing table**. It's strong enough to hold a sewing machine and because it's higher than a regular table, sit on a stool and you won't strain your back as much. There are lots of drawers and space for storing small sewing items.
+ Use as a **craft station** for children.
+ Turn into a **workstation** for a computer.

(?) **DID YOU KNOW?** *Phthalates are chemicals that increase the flexibility of plastics. But there are concerns about their health effects, particularly with babies. Parents who want to reduce their baby's exposure to phthalates should avoid using baby lotions or powders in plastic packaging. No issue had been found with dummies, plastic toys or baby creams in metal tubes or pots. There are new concerns, however, about bisphenol A or PBA, the plastics that whiten when you bend them.*

TIP: It's best not to keep old plastic baby bottles. Throw them out if they discolour or develop cracks (leaving sparkles) or scratches. They are no longer hygienic and bacteria can thrive. Milk allows bacteria to grow quickly. Shannon prefers glass bottles: shatterproof varieties are now available.

Playing

You don't need lots of money to keep kids entertained. Instead, use some resourcefulness and creativity. Kids love pulling things apart to see how they work and then putting them back together in new and unusual ways. Encourage them to make contraptions and set challenges. Even if you have boxes of toys, try out some of these old-fashioned play ideas.

How to make a busy box

Fill a container (such as an old fruit box or document box) with items such as egg cartons, wrapping paper, feathers, fabric, wool, string, ribbons, buttons, punnets, old toothbrushes, broken toys and just about anything that can be turned into something else. Save for a rainy day or that I'm-bored moment.

TIP: Get into the habit of putting plastic sheeting down before starting any messy activities. This will protect surfaces and make cleaning easier.

How to make secret notes

Dip a paintbrush or a knitting needle in lemon juice and paint pictures or write a message on a sheet of paper and allow it to dry. When the paper is heated in a microwave (heat in 10-second bursts), the message is revealed! Egg white works in the same way.

How to make pirate paper

This activity requires some adult supervision. Paint
the edge of a sheet of paper with cold black tea and
carefully burn the edges with a lit candle (the paper is
wet from the tea so it will singe rather than burst into
flame). Then add your secret message using lemon
juice. The message can be revealed using a magnifying
glass in the sun. Another way to make pirate paper is
to make a weak solution of instant coffee and water.
Wipe the solution over a sheet of paper and put it in an
oven on the lowest heat for around 15 minutes or until
the paper starts to curl at the edges.

TIP: Get kids to make invitations for their parties.
It's fun and will save money.

How to make your own paint

You'll need to buy tempera, a powder paint sold
in art supply stores. To make finger paint, combine
2 tablespoons of cornflour and 6 tablespoons of cold
water and mix well. Add 1½ cups of boiling water
and continue to stir until thick. Add the tempera
powder. Allow to cool then store in the fridge to use
when the creative mood strikes. To make brush paint,
mix 4 parts tempera powder to 8 parts water and
1 part dishwashing liquid.

How to make your own tenpin bowling alley
Collect 10 shampoo or conditioner bottles. Put some
sand in the bottom to weight them and turn them into
pins. Find a flat area for the bowling alley, arrange the
pins and use a tennis ball as the bowling ball.

TIP: Teach your children the value of money. Have
a list of weekly chores—such as cleaning their
room, unloading the dishwasher, cleaning their
teeth or doing homework—and pay a certain
amount of pocket-money per task to show them
that reward involves work. They'll learn to
appreciate gifts more and get a perspective on
how much things cost in relation to time spent
doing chores. For example, they can work out
how many hours it takes to buy a Playstation.

TIP: Help your children learn the value of recycling
and make a bit of money by collecting aluminium
cans. Use a magnet to determine if something is
made with aluminium or tin. A magnet will stick
to tin.

SAVE: OLD TOYS
OTHER USES:
+ It's best to **pass on** old toys or **donate** them to
charity.

+ Organise a **toy swap party** with friends and family or sell them on the internet.
+ Keep the wheels from ride-on toys to **reuse**.
+ Keep rubberised handle covers from bike handles and use them on **garden tools**.
+ Many old toys can be pulled apart and turned into **new contraptions** or inventions. Keep the parts in the kids' busy box.

TIP: If your child has allergies, put soft toys in the freezer each month for 12 hours to kill dust mites. Then wash and place in the sun to dry.

TIP: When Jennifer was in primary school, everyone had a homemade fabric chair cover with a pocket in the back for storing books. It's a nifty idea if storage is limited at your place.

DID YOU KNOW? *In the US, eco-daycare centres are opening up. The centres don't allow PVC products, only have natural and organic toys, the floors emit radiant heat and they are cleaned with environmentally friendly products.*

SAVE: CRAYON STUBS

OTHER USES:

+ Use crayons to **repair scratches** on marble and CaesarStone benchtops. Match the colour and rub over the affected area. The wax in the crayons will fill and smooth the scratch.

+ Collect all the tail end crayon stubs and place them in the toe of a pair of pantyhose. Tie off tightly, then draw on paper to **make rainbow patterns**. This is easy for little hands to use.

+ Make **stained-glassed window paper**. Put the crayon bits over paper and then zap in the microwave in short bursts until the wax melts. Leave to harden. You'll end up with a translucent multi-coloured piece of paper.

TIP: To remove crayon marks from walls, dampen an eraser in a bowl of soapy water and rub over the mark. The wax in the crayon will roll off in balls. If needed, put bicarb on a damp cotton bud and wipe over the mark. Use an old toothbrush and bicarb for a large mark. You could also add a few drops of tea tree oil to a damp cloth and wipe over the mark. To remove crayon marks from wallpaper, rub with a piece of brown bread.

 DID YOU KNOW? *If you are concerned about any of your children's toys (including antique toys) containing lead, use a lead-testing kit available from paint stores.*

SAVE: SPORTING GOODS

OTHER USES:

+ **Donate** old sporting goods to charities, schools or kindergartens.

+ If they're damaged, show the children how to cut broken footballs and tennis balls in half and turn them into a **slug trap**. To do this, put beer inside the cut ball and place in the garden. The slugs will be attracted to the beer, fall into it and drown.

+ Turn old netballs into **bird feeders**. Thread string through the valve so it can be hung up. Then cut a hole in one side of the netball. Put birdseed inside and the birds can feed from it.

How to fix a puncture on a bike

There's no need to buy a new tube for your tyre because it's easy to patch over punctures. You will need a puncture kit that includes special glue and rubber patches. But first, you need to find where the puncture is. The easiest way is to put the damaged tube in a tub of water and watch where it bubbles. That's where the hole is. If you can't find the hole, add dishwashing liquid to the tub and the bubbles will be bigger. Once you've located the hole, use the contents of your puncture kit and you'll be back on your bike in no time.

SAVE: SKATEBOARDS

OTHER USES:

+ Use them to **move furniture** and heavy items.
+ Remove the wheels and use them to make a **billycart**. You can also use the wheels from

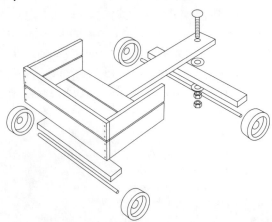

rollerskates in a similar way. Shannon used to make a billycart using a wooden fruit box, timber paling, two sets of wheels on axles, rope or string, hammer and nails and 1 bolt. Look for all the bits you'll need in council clean-ups.

Gardening

Kids love to watch plants grow. Help them develop a green thumb.

How to grow carrot tops
You'll need:

cotton balls
plastic tray (reuse one from fruit and vegetable packaging)
cut carrot tops

Place the cotton balls on the plastic tray. Put the carrot tops, cut-side down, on the cotton balls and place on a sunny windowsill. Have your child add water each day so the cotton balls remain damp. After about a week, watch as the top of the carrot sprouts green foliage.

You could also scatter some snow pea sprouts or alfalfa seeds on the cotton balls. The kids can eat the sprouts.

How to make a garden in a bowl

Your garden could be as compact as a salad bowl.
All you need is a large plastic bowl, some sand for
drainage and some soil. Plant anything small and
low-growing, such as nasturtiums, violas, pansies,
violets or salvia.

TIP: To graft African violets, remove every third leaf,
dip the broken stems in hormone or rooting
powder (available from the nursery) and bury each
stem in potting mix. They'll create new African
violets, and your original plant will also produce
more flowers. If you plant two different varieties
together, put the stems into hormone or rooting
powder side by side to create a new flower.

How to press flowers

It's fun for children to keep their favourite flowers
forever by pressing them. Arrange fresh flowers on
a sheet of paper: it's best not to have anything
overlapping. Remember, how you place them is how
they will look when they're dried. Put another sheet of
paper on top. Place the paper and flowers in the middle
of a thick, heavy book: the more weight on top, the
better. It will take about 3 days for the flowers to dry.
You can also dry flowers in quick bursts in the
microwave. To do this, arrange the flowers between two

sheets of microwave-safe paper (as described above) and place in an old paperback book. Make sure the book doesn't have staples or you'll get arcing in the microwave. Zap in the microwave in 30-second bursts until dried. Use them as you like!

WHY IT MATTERS: The most recent report from the World Glacier Monitoring Service has found glaciers are melting faster than at any time since records began. Glaciers feed river systems so their decline will mean water shortages, rising sea levels, increased flooding, avalanches and drought. Not good!

How to organise kids

One of the easiest ways to organise kids is to use a noticeboard. Buy one or make your own from old corks (see page 42–3). Get into the habit of hanging any school notes or other paraphernalia from it. It means there's a one-stop shop for information about school projects, excursions and events. Organise schoolwork using old cereal boxes as files. Have one as a base box and use the other as a lid. Decorate in any way you like. Create 'stash spots' under the bed where they can store items in old polystyrene fruit boxes.

Clothing and shoes

Babies' and children's clothing has to be incredibly tough and durable to handle all that wear and tear. One way to extend the life of clothes is to add panels. For example, if they've outgrown their jeans, cut them off and make them into shorts or unpick the outer side seams and add a panel or some braid. If the neckline of a T-shirt is worn, you can get replacement binding that can be sewn on by machine or hand. Patch over holes and tears with heart, star or animal shapes, appliqués or logos. Rocket shapes and dinosaur shapes are easy to cut out. Sew on or use iron-on adhesive. Patch the knees of trousers with old windcheater material before they are worn.

Clothes in good condition can be passed on or donated to charity. Worn clothes can be converted into patching fabric or rags for the rag bag.

TIP: Knowing some sewing basics will help you save money because making costumes for school plays or concerts is so much cheaper than buying them. Do a sewing course (take your children along – it's a fun thing to do together). Ask at fabric shops or sewing machine shops.

Babies

SAVE: CLOTH NAPPIES

OTHER USES:

+ The cotton used in cloth nappies is really good quality so don't throw them away. Shannon often buys them at garage sales to use as **cleaning rags**.

+ Turn into **washers**. They're soft enough to wash a baby's face (or bottom!).

SAVE: DISPOSABLE NAPPIES

OTHER USES:

+ If it's only been peed on, it can be used to **protect seedlings**. When planting, place a used nappy in the bottom of the hole you've dug in the garden bed and plant on top of it. The nappy operates like water crystals and helps retain water.

Cloth versus disposable nappies

As we wrote in *How to be Comfy*, there's an ongoing debate about whether cloth or disposable nappies are better for the environment. Results vary depending on whether you include the impact of using just the nappies or if you also include the production and the disposal of the nappies. There is no easy answer. The University of Queensland investigated the issue and findings suggest that disposable nappies use more energy, land area and solid waste but cloth nappies use more water. The researchers suggest that regardless of the type of nappy you choose, think of ways you can reduce your environmental footprint. It may be a moot point with *Choice* reporting that in 2001, 89 per cent of all nappies changed in Australia are disposable, up from 40 per cent in 1993. If you are using disposable nappies, be aware that environmentally friendly options are available that are biodegradable, chlorine free and the plastic is derived from starch.

The more environmentally friendly cloth nappy options include organic cotton, hemp and bamboo. Bamboo and hemp are more absorbent than cotton but hemp nappies require more washing when you first start using them. The greater absorbency also means they can become a bit smelly. You're advised not to use fabric softeners or barrier creams because they create a water-repellent layer. If you use them, there's an extra stage of washing in hot water with dishwashing liquid before putting the nappies in the washing machine. Regardless of the type of cloth, using cloth nappies is cheaper than buying disposable nappies. And if the thought of washing cloth nappies is more than you can bear, nappy services are available.

Most modern designer cloth nappies don't need to be soaked. Just shake the solids into the toilet before placing the nappy in a sealed nappy bucket to await washing. Don't leave them in the bucket for more than a day because urine can affect the fabric. Nappies are unlikely to have greasy stains on them, so use less detergent when washing and opt for an enzyme-free detergent to avoid residue build-up and nappy rash.

If you like to wash with bicarb, white vinegar or essential oils but have a new-style nappy, check that these won't affect its elasticity. Don't be seduced by antibacterial products: they aren't necessary when cleaning nappies and could even lead to antibiotic resistance. It's best to dry nappies on the clothesline where the sun sterilises and removes stains. It's also gentler on the nappy fibres so they'll last longer.

On the issue of cost, estimates vary. Here's a comparison: a basic pack of 10 terry cloth nappies costs $34.95 and a baby would require three sets at a cost of $104.85. Estimated washing costs are $50 per year. Basic disposables cost approximately 35 cents each. With seven changes a day, the total cost is $894.25 a year. Also remember that both need nappy liners, wipes, covers, etc. as well. Choose what works for you. There's plenty of information on the internet to help with this decision.

TIP: To disguise the smell of a nappy bucket, mix 2 tablespoons of bicarb, $\frac{1}{2}$ teaspoon of dried sage, $\frac{1}{2}$ teaspoon of dried thyme and 2 drops of lavender oil on a saucer and place near the bucket.

TIP: If you buy disposable nappies in bulk, turn the big, brightly coloured box into a toy box. It's made of dense cardboard and is very sturdy.

TIP: Get into the habit of washing new babies' clothing before they're worn to remove chemicals such as formaldehyde and toxic starches.

How to store baby clothes

The smallest amount of bacteria can grow when an item sweats in plastic so it's best not to store baby clothes in plastic bags because no matter how well they're laundered they'll tend to go yellow and become smelly. Instead, store them in old cotton pillowcases with a cake of soap or a wardrobe sachet. If using vacuum storage bags, it's a good idea to put clothes into pillowcases first to prevent them yellowing. If you do get yellow marks, deal with them according to the fabric. With cotton, make a paste of NapiSan Plus, paint it on the stain, leave for 20 minutes and wash. For woollens, use cheap shampoo and blood-heat water, rinse and dry flat in the shade.

Older kids

How to extend the life of school uniforms

School uniforms are designed to withstand lots of wear but you can help make them last as long as possible. With boys, add knee patches inside their trousers. With girls, make sure there's a generous hem on their tunics and skirts and let them down as they grow. To remove a hemline mark, apply white vinegar to a cloth and wipe on both sides of the hemline then iron with a warm iron. If you're not sure how to sew a hem, see page 217 in *How to be Comfy*. Many schools have polo shirts as part of the uniform. To keep them stain free, spray with scotchguard before they wear them.

How to clean a school bag

It's easy for school bags to accumulate dirt. For cloth bags, remove all the contents, go outside, turn the bag inside out, shake clean then hang on the clothesline to air. For non-cloth or plastic bags, clear the contents and vacuum, making sure you get right into the corners. Wipe with dishwashing liquid and water. Hang upside down on the clothesline to dry completely and prevent mould from developing.

How to make a smock

These are really handy to throw over and protect clothes when the creative mood strikes. Use an old business shirt and remove the collar and cuffs. Fold over the fabric at the cuffs and collar, and hem with a running stitch. Then thread elastic through using a safety pin. Wear the smock with the buttons at the back.

How to make shoes last for longer

When buying new shoes, have your child wear a thick pair of socks. As their feet grow, use thinner socks until it's time for a newer, bigger pair of shoes. Most school shoes also come with rubberised inserts that can be removed when the child's feet grow. Another idea is to add sheepskin inserts to the new shoes and as the child's feet grow, remove and replace the inserts with thinner felt liners.

 DID YOU KNOW? *In days gone by, tissue paper was often stuffed into the toe of a too-large shoe.*

How to clean leather shoes

When Shannon was young, it was her job to clean the family's shoes on a Saturday morning. Her technique not only cleans the shoes but treats them as well. She was taught to apply shoe polish cleaner with a brush and then leave the shoes in the sunshine. That way, the leather absorbs the polish. When the polish dries, remove the excess with a brush, then buff the shoes with some felt to give them shine.

TIP: Shoelaces will last longer if you run them over a piece of beeswax before threading them into the shoes.

Laundry

Doing the laundry today is easy when compared with days gone by. You separate whites and colours, toss one of the bundles into the washing machine, add detergent and come back in half an hour. Our grandmothers and great-grandmothers had to perform each part of the washing cycle by hand. They'd start by filling a huge copper pot with buckets of water. Then they'd light the kindling beneath the pot and bring the water to the boil. High alkaline lye soap would be added to the washing and they'd use a broom handle or paddle to stir the clothes, just like a human agitator. The dripping garments were then transferred to rinse water and put through a wringer ready to be hung on the clothesline. It was a very unpleasant chore—even worse if the wind was blowing or it was a cold day. We've got nothing to complain about!

You can help the planet by choosing phosphate-free and petrochemical-free washing powder, using smaller quantities, using cold or tepid water in the washing machine and diverting greywater to the garden. You can also lower your electricity bill by avoiding the dryer: hang your washing on the clothesline instead!

SAVE FEATURE: Keep old plastic clothes baskets to store out-of-season clothes (winter clothes in summer and summer clothes in winter). They're ideal because insects aren't attracted to the plastic (the way they are to cardboard), the mesh along the sides allows air to circulate, they're a manageable size and easy to move around. Line the basket with an old sheet (so that the plastic doesn't fume and stain the clothes) before adding the clothes.

Washing and drying

Washing machines

When you buy a washing machine, there are two price tags. The first price tag, or sticker price, is the cost of buying the machine. The second price tag estimates how much water and electricity the machine uses per year and is indicated by energy efficiency stickers. The rating system uses a scale of one to six stars—the more stars the better. It also includes how many kilowatt hours per year the appliance used when tested to the Australian Standard—the lower the number the better. You can estimate how much the appliance will cost per year by multiplying the energy rating guide by the kilowatts per hour. To find the most energy efficient machines, visit www.energyrating.gov.au.

Another important thing to consider when choosing a washing machine is how well it cleans. There's no point in buying a cheap machine if it doesn't clean properly and leaves lint all over your clothes. In

Australia, *Choice* magazine compares the performance of different washing machines and their reports can be purchased (see their website, www.choice.com.au). Another way to find out how well a washing machine performs is to ask for other people's experiences. Talk to friends and family or visit online discussion forums.

TIP: Make sure the washing machine has a filter or it won't rinse properly.

Front loader versus top loaders

What you choose is a matter of preference. Shannon loves her top loader because she can interrupt the cycle and be in control of the wash and there's less back bending when loading and unloading. Jennifer loves her front loader because it's compact and has many cleaning options.

Front loaders use 40 per cent less water (by cycling clothes through water at the bottom of the drum whereas top loaders fill the entire drum with water). A 7-kilogram front loader uses around 60 litres of water per wash. A 7-kilogram top-loader uses about 120 litres of water per wash. Front loaders also remove more water in the spin cycle so garments need less time drying.

TIP: Many modern washing machines have a 'delay start' function so you can program them to run when water is off-peak and therefore cheaper.

DID YOU KNOW? *Front loader washing machines use specific low-sudsing detergents, as Jennifer discovered the hard way. Running her brand new front loader empty for its first wash (as instructed), she used the usual powder only to find the laundry floor covered in soap suds. A quick call to the hotline uncovered the problem and she was advised to remove the suds by adding 1 cup of full cream milk to the dispenser. The suds still inside the machine dissipated immediately. She now uses an appropriate detergent!*

TIP: If you use cold water in your washing machine, you save around $1 per load.

TIP: If you soak clothes in a bucket (with or without washing powder) before putting them in the washing machine, you can choose a lighter cycle on your washing machine. Empty the bucket of water (and its contents) into the machine to use less fresh water. You could even use the water collected in a bucket when you shower.

Laundry detergents

Be mindful when selecting laundry detergents,
particularly if you use greywater or if anyone in the
family has sensitive skin. Avoid ones that are high in
phosphorous (it causes algal blooms) and salt and
those with petrochemical-based ingredients. Opt for
plant-based detergents that are fully biodegradable.
And don't be seduced by claims of extra cleaning
power. It generally means more chemicals are added
to the detergent mix. Instead, to whiten clothes, add
½ cup of lemon juice to your rinse cycle and hang out
the clothes in the sunshine. You can also buy eco-balls
or laundry-balls that use mineral pellets. These work by
altering water molecules and don't produce soap suds
so you can skip the rinse cycle when washing.

Shannon suggests using half the quantity of your
regular detergent and adding bicarb to the wash cycle
and white vinegar to the rinse cycle (placed in the
fabric-softener slot) in the washing machine. For a
large top loader, add ½ cup of bicarb and ½ cup of
white vinegar. For a small top loader, add 2 tablespoons
of bicarb and 2 tablespoons of white vinegar. For a
large front loader, add 2 tablespoons of bicarb and
2 tablespoons of white vinegar. For a small front
loader, add 1 tablespoon each of bicarb and white
vinegar. Or try these other recipes:

Shannon's recipe for laundry detergent

This recipe is designed for delicates, soft woollens and anything fine. Mix ½ cup of pure soap flakes, ¼ cup of very cheap shampoo, 2 teaspoons of bicarb and 2 teaspoons of white vinegar in a clean (re-labelled) detergent bottle. Add 2 litres of water and shake. It's ready to use. Add fragrance, such as 2 teaspoons of lavender oil, but be careful adding eucalyptus oil because it strips colour and oils from fabric. Adding ½ teaspoon of tea tree oil is a good disinfectant and antiviral.

Shannon's recipe for sensitive skin laundry detergent

Combine 1 tablespoon of pure soap flakes, the juice of 1 lemon and 2 tablespoons of bicarb in a large jar, add 2 cups of warm water and mix well. Label the jar.

TIP: Don't overuse pre-wash treatments.

SAVE: *LIQUID LAUNDRY DETERGENT BOTTLES*

OTHER USES:

+ Most manufacturers have **refill** packs so you can reuse the same container over and over again.
+ Cut along the top and **create a scoop** for the garden or for cleaning kitty litter trays.(See photo on page 15.)
+ Use to **store your own laundry detergent** concoctions (don't forget to label them).

TIP: Keep a funnel (made from the top of an old drink
bottle) in the laundry to pour detergent into
other containers. This is particularly useful if you
buy in bulk.

SAVE: CARDBOARD WASHING POWDER BOXES

OTHER USES:

+ Keep **papers** in them. Because the cardboard is
  impregnated with detergent it keeps bugs away.

TIP: As described in *Speedcleaning*, make your own
starch from rice water. Keep the water after
boiling rice. Mix 1 cup of the rice-water starch
with 2 cups of water and stir thoroughly. Add
½ cup of this mixture to the rinse cycle of the
washing machine. It's great for sheets and lasts
for about a month.

SAVE: GREYWATER

OTHER USES:

+ Rinse water can be collected in a tub and reused.
  If your tub is big enough, collect the rinse water
  and place your inlet hose in the tub for the **next
  load of washing**. Then return the inlet hose to the
  tap before the rinse cycle starts.
+ Collect greywater and reuse it on the **garden or in
  the toilet**. Just be careful with vegetable patches

and make sure no soap water gets into the
waterways (phosphorous and salt in waterways
is a problem). It's more convenient to have a
greywater system professionally installed, but
you can also use a bucket.

 DID YOU KNOW? *According to the Australian
Bureau of Statistics, 24.4 per cent of Australian
households collected greywater in the laundry in
2007.*

How to use the very last drop

It can be frustrating not to use the absolute last
skerrick of a product. To get the last bit of liquid
laundry detergent from a bottle, Shannon removes the
label and places the bottle in the top loader washing
machine. It means all the liquid is used and the bottle
is clean and ready for its next use. To get the very last
drop from liquid soaps or soap-based products, add
1 teaspoon of white vinegar and 1 tablespoon of water
and shake. If using this trick to get the dregs from
Pine-o-Cleen or Solyptol bottles, use the mixture
within 2 hours because it grows bacteria. Never add
vinegar to anything containing chlorine bleach or you'll
get a nasty chemical reaction. Instead, just add water.
To find out if the product contains chlorine, check the
list of ingredients.

TIP: If colour runs from one garment into others in your wash, use the proprietary product Runaway. It comes in two varieties: Runaway for Whites and Coloursafe Runaway.

Dry-cleaning

Dry-cleaning is expensive and damaging to the environment. Many garments sent to the dry-cleaner can be hand washed. It's common for clothing manufacturers to include a 'dry-clean only' label so they're not liable for damage but some of these garments can be washed by hand. The exception is structured clothing, which has defined seams and should go to a dry-cleaner. With fabrics such as rayon, silk or viscose, do a test first by rubbing a wet cotton bud into a seam and leave it to dry. If the fabric crinkles, it can't be hand washed. Be careful with darker coloured rayon, silk and viscose garments which may lose colour if hand washed. You can hand wash wool, linen, cashmere and cotton.

Hand washing

When hand washing, spot clean any stains first (see pages 200–3 in *How to be Comfy* for a quick stain removal guide). Then fill a laundry tub or bucket with blood-heat water and add a small quantity of cheap shampoo. Gently wash the garment by hand, then rinse in clean blood-heat water. The temperature of the rinse water must be the same as the temperature of the wash water. Allow the garment to drain then lay it flat on a towel in the shade to dry. Don't wring out the garment. Iron on a cool setting with lots of steam.

TIP: Minimise visits to the dry-cleaner by airing your clothes outside away from direct sunlight (heat sets stains) before returning to the cupboard. Another way to avoid the dry-cleaner is not to buy clothes with a 'dry-clean only' label.

SAVE: PLASTIC CLOTHES BASKETS
OTHER USES:
+ Clothes baskets are designed to be picked up by one person, which makes them great for **carrying multiple items** at once, such as pots in the garden.
+ Place them in the back of the car and **carry your shopping** from the car to the kitchen in one go.
+ Use as **space helmets or turtle shells** for the kids.

SAVE: OLD WASHING MACHINE
OTHER USES:
+ If the machine still works, find a **new home** for it.
+ If it's broken, **call a repairer**.
+ If it's beyond repair, you can **pull the machine apart**. The drum is easy to remove with a

screwdriver and makes an excellent pot for the garden. Because the inner skin is perforated and the outside isn't, it can hold water away from the roots, acting like a slow watering system.

+ If you don't want it, contact your local council or a **scrap metal recycler** (they can be found in the Yellow Pages). A second-hand dealer might want it for parts.

SAVE: *LAUNDRY TUBS*
OTHER USES:

+ The plug hole in a concrete or metal laundry tub makes them perfect to use for **growing plants in the garden** because draining is as easy as pulling out the plug (Shannon puts the plug on the underside so it's easy to remove). You also avoid weeds because the tub is off the ground and weeds can't spread as easily in a contained environment. If you suspend the tub on a wooden frame, there's space underneath to keep plants such as ferns, orchids and potatoes. And if you're growing herbs, the height makes it easier to pick them. You'll need to water the contents more often if it's a metal rather than concrete tub.

+ Use to **mix fertilisers**. Place a bucket underneath the plug hole, remove the plug (fixed on the underside) and you're ready to go.

+ Use for **worm farms**. Put in the vegetable matter, add a layer of worms and let them do their work. Worm castings are great fertiliser. Put a bucket underneath the drain hole, undo the plug (fixed on the underside) and collect the castings. Use over the garden. For details on worm farms see page 261.

SAVE: PEGS

OTHER USES:

+ Shannon carries a couple of pegs in her handbag in case she needs to **clip** anything, such as a tablecloth flapping in the wind at a café.
+ Use to **seal opened packets of food**. Roll the top of the packet over several times to eliminate air.

TIP: Shannon thinks it's a good idea to wash your plastic and wooden pegs under clean water each week in case birds, bats, spiders or other insects have pooped on them.

TIP: Plastic pegs leave less of a mark on clothes than wooden ones but they break down more quickly from exposure to the sun. Keep in a bucket in the shade when not in use.

WHY IT MATTERS: One of the effects of rising temperatures is less sea ice, which is having an impact on the walrus population. There's not enough Arctic Circle ice for the walruses to share during swimming breaks so they huddle on the shore in large numbers. If the walruses are disturbed, it can set off a stampede. Over 3000 walruses were killed in this way in 2007.

SAVE: LAUNDRY TROLLEY

OTHER USES:

+ Create a small wheelbarrow to **cart items**.
+ Turn it into a **drying rack**. To make some extra cross bars, flatten coat-hanger wire and secure it over the top edge of the trolley. Then peg your clothes to it. It has the added advantage of being easily wheeled out of the way.

How to make a rag bag

The easiest way to make a rag bag is to hang an old pillowcase from two hooks on the back of a door. Put old tea towels, clothes, towels and fabric inside. Some items might need modification, such as removing the gusset and elastic from old underpants and removing zippers, stiff shirt necks and any buttons (keep them in your button box). It will be easier to find the right type of fabric if you keep similar types together. For example, store cotton on one side of the rag bag, polyester on the other and wool in the middle.

TIP: Wool is great for cleaning French polished items and brass but not for cleaning polyurethane.

Dryers

Only use a dryer if you absolutely have to. Hanging clothes in the sun is the best way to dry them because UV light is a great antibacterial. Clothes dried in a dryer wear out faster than clothes dried in the sun because the direct heat and tossing action places more stress on the fibres. The fibres are further strained when they go from a hot to a cold environment really quickly. And, of course, there's the higher electricity bill to consider. For example, a pair of jeans that have been worn one day a week for 4 years, washed after every third wear in a high energy machine at 40°C, tumble dried and then ironed uses 240 kilowatts of energy a year. That's the same as using 4000 60-watt light bulbs for an hour. If you want to save the planet, wear your jeans two days a week, air them on the clothesline and wash them after you have worn them five times.

If you must use the dryer, speed up the drying process by adding a dry tea towel or hand towel to increase the surface area. Another option is to remove most of the moisture by hanging the clothes in the sun (or an airing rack) and then finish the clothes off in the dryer on a low heat. Alternatively, begin by using the dryer until the contents are almost dry and then finish drying them on an airing rack.

 DID YOU KNOW? *Before the 1930s, most people only had two sets of clothes but several sets of under-clothes and used a clothes brush to remove the dust and dirt from the day. Only wealthy people had several changes of clothes.*

SAVE: OLD DRYERS
OTHER USES:

+ If it's still working, **pass it on, sell it** or take the dryer to a second-hand dealer.
+ If it's broken, pull the machine apart and **reuse** various parts. Use the drum as a pot for plants. It already has a hole in the bottom to make draining easy.
+ **Recycle it**. Contact your council or a scrap-metal recycler.

SAVE: DRYER LINT
OTHER USES:

+ Keep lint from your dryer and use it as **stuffing in toys** or as **packing around delicate items**. Keep adding to it until you have enough! Shannon stores hers in a small wastepaper bin with a lid.

> **WHY IT MATTERS:** An OECD report estimates that around 150 million people in the world's biggest cities could be at risk from flooding by 2070. The locations in danger include Calcutta, Mumbai, Bangladesh, China, Vietnam, Thailand, Myanmar and Miami.

Ironing

Many people don't iron their clothes at all and apply the 'wash and wear' principle. Realistically, you can't throw away the iron but there are a few things you can do to reduce its use. First, hang the washing as flat as possible to minimise creases. Second, put some aluminium foil under the ironing board cover to increase the amount of heat generated. Finally, try Shannon's lavender oil technique. Fill a spray bottle with 1 litre of water and add ½ teaspoon of lavender oil. Spray this mixture over your clothes before you put them on and they'll become smoother. Use it instead of an ironing aid.

TIP: Always buy a good iron. When it breaks, recycle the metal plate at a scrap-metal recycler. We don't suggest using it to hold a door open. Modern irons don't have the same rustic appeal, or weight, of the old ones.

TIP: If the steam jets in your iron become clogged with mineral deposits, clean them by filling the iron with equal parts white vinegar and water. Let the mixture sit for 1 hour, then empty it out, rinse with clean water and let it steam.

SAVE: *IRONING BOARD*

OTHER USES:

+ A good ironing board should last a lifetime. Shannon still uses an ironing board given to her as a wedding present. Replace the ironing board cover every three years or as required. If you do decide to upgrade, **pass on** your old one to someone who's setting up home.

+ If it's made of iron or steel and starts to go rusty, **fix with Rust Converter** (converts rust into a moisture-free black surface). When doing this, make sure you wear gloves and don't sand the surface first. When converted, apply spray-on enamel paint.

Cleaning

SAVE: *OLD VACUUM CLEANER*

OTHER USES:

+ Use in the garden to **collect stink bugs**!

+ It's handy to use as a **leaf sucker** (rather than using a leaf blower) in the garden. Only suck things smaller than the tube but keep the vacuum away from any liquid. If sucking leaves, cut a hole in the centre of an ice-cream container and tape it to the end of the vacuum cleaner tube, creating a wide mouth. Cut the legs from a pair of pantyhose and tie the cut-off tops of the legs together so you've created an elasticised sack. Place the elastic over the outside edge of the bucket so the crotch of the panythose sits over the vacuum tube hole. That way you can suck up leaves until they fill the pantyhose and empty it into your compost bin or green bin.

+ Use it to **vacuum the car**.

SAVE: INDOOR BROOMS

OTHER USES:

+ If the bristles of the broom are flat, **replace the head**. Use the old head as a boot scraper. See page 12 in *How to be Comfy* for details.

+ **Use as a mop**. Wrap an old damp T-shirt over a broom head and use it to clean the floor. Wash the T-shirt and use over and over again.

SAVE: OLD BUCKETS

OTHER USES:

+ Turn them into **pot plant holders**.
+ Use as **clutter buckets** for cleaning. When cleaning a room, put everything that doesn't belong in the room into the clutter bucket and place outside the room. Clean the room and then return the items in the clutter bucket to their designated place. It's quicker than taking each item back separately.
+ **Store string** in small beach buckets and cover the

top with an old shower cap with a hole in the middle and pull the string out.

+ Use to store **kids' toys**.

Medicine cabinet

A well-stocked medicine cabinet is a must in every household. Keep an eye on use-by dates and return any expired pharmaceuticals or bottles to the chemist to dispose of properly. They can become toxic when out of date and are not good for landfill.

SAVE: *BANDAGES*

OTHER USES:

+ **Reuse** them. Any bandage that's had contact with blood, pus or other bodily wastes needs to be washed in soap and cold water and then washed in boiling water for 3 minutes. Hang on the clothesline to dry. To re-roll a bandage, lay a butter knife along one edge and roll it up by turning the handle.

SAVE: *OLD ASPIRIN (PAST THE USE-BY DATE)*

OTHER USES:

+ Aspirin is a **preservative**. To preserve passionfruit, oranges, lemons or mandarins, add 1 aspirin and 1 teaspoon of sugar to ½ cup of fruit pulp. Stir, place in the fridge and keep for up to 3 weeks.
+ **Keep moths from your garden**. Dissolve 2 aspirins

in 1 litre of water and spray over leafy vegetables.

+ Inhibit the growth of bacteria in **cut flowers** by adding 1 teaspoon of dissolved aspirin to the vase water.

SAVE: VASELINE

OTHER USES:

+ In addition to softening chafed lips, Vaseline is an **instant shoe polish**. It gets rids of cracks in leather and is suitable for any coloured shoe.
+ Lubricate **sticky drawers**.
+ Rub over **nails** before hammering. They will be easier to hammer and the nails won't rust.
+ Wipe over the top edges of outdoor pots or over the top of your letterbox to **deter snails and slugs**.

SAVE: VICKS VAPORUB

OTHER USES:

+ Keep **unwanted cats or possums away**. Rub on the underside of rocks in the garden or the underside of your doormat. Vicks VapoRub contains camphorated oils which cats and possums don't like.

Outside

Many Australian gardens used to be modelled on English ones with row upon row of thirsty roses. These days, we're more likely to have a variety of trees and plants with Australian natives playing a prominent role. Modern backyards are making space for worm farms, compost bins and vegetable patches. If you don't have a backyard, there are numerous tips for a balcony or even a windowsill! We also offer suggestions on how to reuse items in your garage and shed which are ideal spaces for storing all the bits and pieces you've saved around the home. Protect outdoor furniture so it lasts for as long as possible.

> **SAVE FEATURE:** Don't throw the old garden hose away. Use it to cover a bucket handle and save your hands. Place a length of hose over the bucket handle and cut it to the appropriate size. Then cut it lengthways along one side, open it out flat and slide it over the handle.

SAVE: OLD DOORS

OTHER USES:

+ Turn a door into a new **table**, as Jennifer did years ago. She bought an old shed door from a recycled timber shop, stripped it and coated it. Her dad added legs using timber stored under the house.

+ Place an old door over trestles when entertaining to create a **buffet or drinks table**.

SAVE: FLYSCREEN

OTHER USES:

+ Use old flyscreen to **cover drains**. Water can still run through the flyscreen but cockroaches and other nasties won't be able to get in.
+ Use old flyscreen to **sift pebbles** from potting mix. Sift the mixture as you would flour. Use the pebbles as mulch to prevent weeds.
+ Use it to **strain paint**.
+ Cover **pet cages**. Don't forget that pets are affected by insects as well.

Smart house design

We're much better these days at designing and building houses that work with the elements. The industry term for this is thermal efficiency (or passive solar design), which looks at the orientation of your house and the type of building materials, insulation, ventilation and glazing used. The idea is that your home maintains a natural temperature between 18–26°C without heating or cooling.

Ways to cut back on energy use in the home include:

→ **Insulation**—line the roof, ceiling, walls and floors with insulation to reduce your air conditioning and heating needs and cut your energy bill.

→ **Windows**—are a source of heat transfer. In the southern hemisphere it's a good idea to place eaves over north-facing windows to help regulate the sun in summer. The sun sits lower in winter and will be able to shine through the window to warm the room. To reduce the impact of summer sun on west-facing windows, use deep eaves, awnings, UV-film or trellises (grapes or wisteria are ideal). Other ways to regulate the temperature and the amount of sun that comes through windows is to plant deciduous trees in front of them or double-glaze them.

→ **Rainwater tanks**—after being banned for many years in urban areas, governments are now encouraging households to install rainwater tanks by providing rebates. You can't drink water from them but they're perfectly fine for watering the garden, washing the clothes or flushing the toilet. They come in a range of sizes and colours. Attach them to your gutters to collect rain.

→ **Greywater diverter systems**—these systems redirect water that goes down the drain in the shower or laundry to the garden. Consult your council to find out the regulations in your area. They need to be professionally installed.

→ **Solar panels**—given the amount of sun we get in Australia, we're mad not to capture it and use it to power our homes. Installing solar panels will help you save money in the long term.

The garden

The more plants and variety you have in the garden, the better it is for the environment. But before racing in with your shovel, work out how you want to use the space and find out which plants work best in your climate. You don't have to limit yourself to decorative plants. Growing fruit and vegetables not only saves money, it means fewer greenhouse gases, less exposure to chemicals, more efficient use of water and an overall sense of satisfaction.

Whatever type of garden you have, use mulch to help prevent weeds and reduce water loss. Mulch can be organic—bark, pea straw, lucerne, straw, sugarcane or shredded newspaper—or inorganic—pebbles or gravel. You could also use compost as mulch. Place over the garden bed to a depth of 5–10 centimetres.

If you don't have a backyard there are still plenty of plants you can grow in pots. Decorate a small garden, deck or balcony with potted bay trees, lemon trees, lime trees, cumquats and miniature oranges or grow your own herbs, watercress, rocket, mignonette lettuce and cherry tomatoes in pots on a windowsill. String a tomato vine along the bottom of the sill. Bunny ball carrots can be grown in a 5-centimetre deep pot on a windowsill. Another option is to join a garden co-op where community land is divided into plots. Talk with your neighbours, work out what you each want to grow and trade the fruit and vegetables you've grown.

There's more range with Australian natives these days.

Many natives have been hybridised and offer great colours that are easy to grow. They require less water and are perfectly adapted to the climate and wildlife: for instance, grevilleas attract birds and helpful insects.

TIP: Save water and have a better fruiting crop by peeing on lemon and orange trees and tomatoes. If your backyard is exposed, pee into a watering can inside and then apply.

 DID YOU KNOW? *A watering can holds 4 litres of water. A sprinkler uses 540 litres of water per hour.*

Shannon's vegie garden

Shannon's vegie patch, which was started from non-irradiated seeds, is only 1.8 x 4.5 metres in size.

Before starting your patch, clear weeds from the area. One easy way to do this is with newspaper: put down four layers, wetting it as you go. Use topsoil, compost, straw and sand in equal parts and scatter over the newspaper until 10 centimetres deep. Using a pitchfork, stab every metre to allow the soil to aerate so you won't get nasty microbes. The newspaper over time will turn into mulch and you'll be left with a great base for your vegie patch. At the time of writing, Shannon had 12 corn plants, 3 zucchini, 4 eggplants, 8 capsicums, 6 cucumbers, 12 beetroot, 12 silverbeet,

12 clumps of carrots, 12 vine tomatoes, 12 broccoli, 12 lettuces, 6 strawberry plants, 1 watermelon and 1 pumpkin vine growing in her vegie patch. She says the flavours are fantastic.

TIP: If your vegie patch is near heavy traffic, wash your picked produce in a sink of water and add 1 teaspoon of white vinegar. After washing, rinse in clean water. Peel any root vegetables.

TIP: For specialist Australian seeds, consult The Digger's Club at www.diggers.com.au. They specialise in non-mainstream seeds and deliver through the post. Jennifer's friends grow heirloom tomatoes in their backyard from these seeds.

TIP: Shannon thinks it's best to remove weeds by hand rather than using weed killer. That way, you don't damage other plants and the process of weeding helps aerate the soil. Mulch is another way of keeping weeds under control. Be vigilant with toxic weeds, such as wandering jew, which can aggravate asthma in children.

How to grow potatoes without digging

If you have the space, here's an easy way to grow potatoes. Stack four or five old tyres (your local garage may have some) on top of each other so they look like a big, tall pot. Fill the interior with topsoil and drill holes along the tyres with a 10-centimetre hole bit. Put potato seeds in the holes and keep them moist but not wet. They take about a year to grow but you'll get a year's worth of potatoes that will last for a year. You can leave grown potatoes in the soil for up to 12 months. If you want a quicker result, use gourmet varieties because they have more eyes (the pointy bits that sprout) and therefore grow faster. After removing the potatoes from the tyre stack, store them in a hessian sack in a cool, dry and dark place.

TIP: Use the garden to colour your lips. Rub some geranium petals on your lips and add Vaseline for gloss. Shannon used to put Vaseline on her eyelashes to darken them.

TIP: Avocado trees take some time to grow but they're worth the wait because they're rich in flavour. They can be trained to grow in small spaces or along a wall espalier-style. To bonsai avocado trees, put the tree in a mesh basket in a pot and trim any roots that grow through the basket—this will stunt its growth but won't affect its ability to fruit. Bonsai avocados are about 25 per cent smaller than regular avocados.

How to grow a sweet potato vine

Chop a sweet potato into four pieces so that each piece has one eye. Bury each piece in 3-centimetre deep soil and add water. If you don't have a garden, use planter boxes or hanging baskets. In less than 3 months you'll have a sweet potato vine. It's easy to cut back and manage and you'll have edible sweet potatoes as well.

TIP: Help roses grow by burying fish heads, tails and guts 10 centimetres beneath the rosebush. As they rot, they feed the rose.

TIP: Keep possums from attacking your vegie patch by mixing 1 teaspoon of chilli powder to 1 cup of olive oil. Wipe around the edges of the patch. Or use Vicks VapoRub.

SAVE: PALM FRONDS

OTHER USES:

+ The heavy part at the bottom of a palm frond is shaped like a dish. When you place it in hot water, it can be moulded into any shape you like. Turn it into **bread baskets or gift baskets**.

+ Trim the frond and take the pod to your local
  florist. They might even give you money for it.
+ The large pod sections can be used to build a
  fairy house. Cut in 30-centimetre lengths, stand
  vertically and staple the corners together to form
  the walls. Bend one frond in half to form a roof
  and staple on top.

TIP: Turn a cut palm tree trunk into a stool or
stepping stones. Use the seeds as mulch as you
would pebbles.

SAVE: PINE TREE CONES
OTHER USES:
+ Dust in glitter and use as **Christmas decorations**.
+ Use as **kindling** for fires.
+ Collect edible **pine nuts** as a green pine cone ripens.

SAVE: PLASTIC PLANT POTS
OTHER USES:
+ Wash in boiled water and **use for seedlings**.

TIP: Jacaranda seed pods make great jewellery and
belt buckles. They have a natural varnish (so
you don't have to seal them) and a lovely gold
interior. The pod can be split into two so you
have matching pairs.

SAVE: GARDEN HOSE

OTHER USES:

+ Use hose to **cover dangerous edges**. For example, large olive oil tins have sharp edges when cut. Place some hose around the edge to form a rubber lip so that you won't cut yourself. When empty, olive oil tins make great wastepaper bins or buckets.

+ Use over **shopping bag handles**. Carrying plastic shopping bags can be hard work for your hands. Keep a 10-centimetre length of hose, slit down one side, in your handbag ready to use.

+ **Cover** items that are likely to rust when exposed to sun and rain. Place hose over the area and it'll last much longer.

+ For arthritis sufferers, put a short length of old hose over a **garden tap** to make it easier to turn.

 DID YOU KNOW? Keep birds away with plastic snakes. You could even recycle old garden hose to look like a snake.

MAKE A CHANGE: A college in the United States is giving new bikes to first-year students who promise not to bring cars to the campus for a year. Students who take up the bribe will get a free mountain bike with lock and helmet.

How to compost

Composting is a great way to save money and help the environment and the rich, crumbly organic matter is fabulous for the garden. Because it's so beneficial, many councils give residents compost kits to encourage their use. If yours doesn't, you can buy compost bins at hardware stores, nurseries and some department stores. The ideal compost bin should be easily accessible (but as far from the house as possible), have no gaps in the sides and be able to be covered with a lid. Keep in the shade because the sun can overheat them. To get the compost started you'll need a mix of acid and alkali plant matter. It's important to allow air to flow so use a variety of contents so the compostable material doesn't clump. Add grass clippings, shredded newspaper, straw and food scraps or anything else that will decay quickly, and turn with a fork every day to aerate. You also need enough, but not too much, water to get the micro-organisms functioning. You may need to add manure or blood and bone to speed up the composting process. The quality of your compost will depend on what you put in it: the broader the range of nutrients, the better. Insects, mice and rats are attracted to rotting food matter (particularly meat and dairy products) so make sure you seal your compost.

TIP: Be careful of stray pumpkin seeds. Jennifer's parents had to remove a rather large pumpkin vine from their yard after a seed started to grow near the compost heap. The vine became out of control very quickly.

Install a worm farm

Another way to get rid of vegetable scraps is to have a worm farm. Visit your council, nursery or hardware store to get a container, worms and instructions. There are three main types of composting worms: tiger worms, Indian worms and red wrigglers. Worm castings are ideal fertiliser.

Worms love most vegetable and fruit scraps except citrus and onions, which contain smelly volatile oils. It's best not to use meat and dairy because they attract flies. Store your worm farm in the shade and cover it with newspaper, hessian or a suitable lid.

TIP: Your local florist might be interested in your excess greenery clippings, such as fishbone ferns, magnolia leaves, camellias, gardenias and banksia fronds, or use them yourself in flower arranging. Put additional material into your compost.

DID YOU KNOW? *During WWII, edible leaves, such as nasturtiums, were used in sandwiches as a substitute for mustard. It's fine to eat pansy and viola flowers but don't eat their leaves because they have a laxative effect.*

DID YOU KNOW? *Fruitwood trees, such as peaches and apples, are lovely to burn in fireplaces and generate a fresh, fragrant smell. If you use them when barbecuing they flavour what you're cooking. Use appropriate timber from your lumber pile or go to a timber mill and use off-cuts but make sure they haven't been treated with arsenic and cyanide. Be careful with the timber you use because some trees, such as oleander, are toxic when burned and camphor laurel makes food taste awful.*

TIP: If you chop a tree down, put it on your verge with a sign 'Free Firewood'. To find out how to treat it, see *How to be Comfy*.

How to basket weave

Use branches from a willow tree to make baskets. Strip the branches and weave them while still green or soak them in a bucket of water until flexible. After weaving, leave in the sun to dry. Grape vines also make great baskets. There are several different designs you can weave and patterns are available on the internet.

WHY IT MATTERS: In January 2002, when the temperature reached 43°C in New South Wales, 3500 flying foxes in nine different colonies were found dead. Scientists believe the deaths were related to climate change. Since 1994 over 30,000 flying foxes have been killed in 19 similar heat-related events.

How to control pests

As Melissa King wrote in our magazine *Home Basics*, companion planting can help attract or repel insects in your garden. Rather than reach for chemicals, look to nature first to control pests:

Garlic around roses deters aphids;

French marigolds repel white fly if you plant them with tomatoes;

Wormwood tea repels flies, fleas and cabbage moths;

Sage and mint protect broccoli, lettuce, cabbage, brussels sprouts, bok choy, etc. from cabbage white butterfly;

Lavender, catmint, geranium and **fennel** confuse pests with their strong smell;

Pyrethrum is an all-round bug repellent. Grow it near your front door or turn into a tincture (see page 40 for instructions);

Chives prevent apple scab in apple trees;

Tansy repels moths, flies and ants;
Fennel deters flies, fleas and ants;
Catnip repels ants, fleas and rats;
Nasturtiums repel aphids and pests attracted to
pumpkins, squash and zucchini;
Ladybirds eat aphids and can be bought from some
nurseries.

How to deter nasties the non-toxic way

There are a range of non-toxic remedies to attract
nasties but we're afraid you'll be left with the icky task
of clearing the bodies. Here are some ways to deter
nasties:

Ants—mix ⅓ cup of molasses, 6 tablespoons of sugar
and 6 tablespoons of active dry yeast. Dip cardboard
strips into the mixture and place in areas where ants
travel. Tie strips of cloth saturated in castor oil around
the legs of tables. Be aware that castor oil smells
horrible. Shannon prefers one part borax to one part
icing sugar for sweet ants and one part borax to one
part Parmesan cheese for savoury ants. Or find the
nest and pour boiling water down it.

Cockroaches—sprinkle salt around the edges of
doorways and windowsills.

Flies—in a saucer, mix 1 teaspoon of cream, 1 teaspoon
of sugar and ½ teaspoon of black pepper and flies will
head straight into it (but it's a slow death). To make

flypaper, mix ¼ cup of golden syrup, 1 tablespoon of brown sugar and 1 tablespoon of sugar. Pour over strips of brown paper and soak overnight. Poke a hole in one end of a strip, insert string and hang up. Lavender oil deters flies: put on a cloth and wipe over doorjambs, under outdoor tables and around windows. Place some cloves in a piece of muslin and hang from light fittings.
Mozzies—apply lavender oil to your wrists or put on a cloth and wipe over doorjambs and windows. Use citronella oil and wipe over doorjambs and windows or add to the burning surface of a candle. Mozzies dislike basil but flies love if so it you have both, use citronella or lavender oil or rub the top burning surface of a candle with lemon oil or orange oil. Plant *Pelargonium citrosum* (citronella) near entertaining areas. You can also crush or shred the leaves and place them in a bowl to deter mozzies.
Slugs and snails—fill the shell of half an orange with beer. The slugs and snails climb in and can't get out. Or pay your children 5 cents for every slug and snail caught and placed in a bucket. Sprinkle them with salt and they will die.

The clothesline

Many Australian homes still have a trusty Hills hoist clothesline planted in the middle of the backyard. If you don't, you probably have one of the modern variations that suit space-challenged backyards. A clothesline of some description is a simple but really important way to help the environment. It's worth making the effort to hang out your washing rather than putting it into the dryer. Hanging clothes on the line cuts energy use, and the UV light from the sun kills bacteria. If your clothes smell stale, airing them outside on the clothesline for an hour or so removes unwanted odours.

 DID YOU KNOW? *People used to put airing racks in their rose gardens to scent their clothes.*

SAVE: *OLD CLOTHESLINE WIRE*

OTHER USES:

+ Old clothesline wire is very good quality so don't throw it away. Keep it in the shed ready for **other uses**.
+ Use it to **fence small areas**.
+ Place it along a fence line to **train sweet peas and beans**.
+ Use it to **hang heavy pictures or mirrors**. Put two pinch clips on the wire to create a loop on either end and screw to the back of the picture frame.

TIP: Snow peas and sugar snap peas are really easy to grow. Plant them in the ground or in pots but make sure you have a frame for them to grow along. An old umbrella frame is ideal. Remove the handle and put the spike into the ground. The peas hang down from the struts, making them easy to pick.

Outdoor furniture

Our temperate climate makes outdoor entertaining a popular option for most of the year. Bear in mind that exposure to sun and rain can reduce the life of your outdoor furniture so coat them in a good sealer. Teak, oak and treated cedar can handle the elements but will fade to silver over time. To prevent this, wipe over them with black tea. A lot of this furniture is collapsible so store it out of the elements when you're not using it. Keep cushions and fabrics under cover in a dry place. If buying new furniture, check that it's been made with timber certified by the Forest Stewardship Council or consider buying second-hand. There are many online listings for second-hand outdoor furniture.

SAVE: OUTDOOR TABLE

OTHER USES:

+ If you don't need your table any more, **give it away or sell it**.
+ If the table is damaged, you can **replace** the legs or top.
+ Lighter tables can be converted to a **potting table**.
+ Remove the top and use it as a **drop table**. Hinge the tabletop to the wall and add prop legs or support chains as needed.

SAVE: OUTDOOR CHAIRS

OTHER USES:

+ **Freshen up** with a coat of paint and new cushions. Try to sell them or give them away.
+ For damaged chairs, use the cushions as **kneeling pads** when gardening.
+ Strip metal-framed chairs and **grow beans or other vines** over them.

DID YOU KNOW? *In an effort to reduce pollution in the lead-up to the Beijing Olympics, authorities banned outdoor kebab sellers who grill their food over wood or coal fires. Organisers of the London 2012 Games want the Olympic flame to use low-carbon fuel.*

SAVE: CANVAS UMBRELLAS

OTHER USES:

+ If the canvas is worn, you can **repair or replace** it. Buy new canvas from fabric or furnishing stores. Timber and metal struts can be repaired using a hand-held rivet gun. Or take the umbrella to a camping supply or sail supply store and they will sew the canvas to size for you. It's cheaper and the quality is better.

+ The umbrella frame can be used to **grow roses** to create a spectacular display in the garden. Remove the canvas and place the stand in the ground. This suits grapes and other vines as well.

+ Create a **greenhouse** by covering the entire frame down to the ground with mosquito netting. Peg the netting to the ground with old tent pegs or refashioned coat-hangers.

SAVE: OLD RAIN UMBRELLAS

OTHER USES:

+ If your umbrella loses its **strut cap** and the fabric is loose, replace it using a plastic plug from the end of a biro. Use a hot needle to pierce the sides of the plug so you can stitch it to the umbrella fabric.

+ Use as a **food cover** when entertaining outside. Remove the fabric on the umbrella, cover the wire frame with cheesecloth or muslin and place it over food. It will keep flies and other nasties away.

+ Put in the **dress-up box**.

+ Turn into a **parasol**. Use a heat gun to glue fabric to the ribs of the parasol and add lace or ruffles to the edge.

+ Use in the garden as a frame to support **sweet peas and beans**.

SAVE: BARBECUES

OTHER USES:

+ With round barbecues, turn the top and bottom into **pots** for plants. You could even turn them into hanging baskets by fixing chains to them. There is the added bonus of drainage holes.

+ Use the grill plate from a round barbecue when **camping**.

+ Strip other barbecues down to their component parts. Grills can be placed under heavy pot plants for extra drainage. Or take the parts to a **recycler**.

TIP: Gas barbecues are more environmentally friendly than charcoal-burning ones.

Recycling bins

In city areas, most homes have four separate bins: one is for general household waste, another is for paper goods, the third for glass, steel and plastic, and the fourth is for green waste. These bins have information stickers which tell you what you can and can't put into them. Most packaging has recycling numbers stamped on it to indicate whether it is acceptable for recycling or not. As a general guide, here's information from one council.

Paper bin
Acceptable material:
 Newspapers and magazines;
 Cardboard products;
 Office paper and envelopes;
 Clean cardboard food containers/cartons;
 Advertising material (junk mail);
 Telephone books;
 Empty pizza boxes;
 Egg cartons.
Unacceptable material:
 Plastic bags;
 Pizza boxes with food inside;
 Food-soiled paper and cardboard;
 Bubble wrap;

Waxed cardboard;
Milk and juice cartons;
Polystyrene.

Co-mingled bin

Acceptable items:
  Glass bottles and jars*;
  Steel and aluminium cans;
  Milk and juice cartons;
  Aerosol cans (remove lids);
  PET/plastic bottles marked 1, 2, 3, 4, 5 and R;
  Ice-cream, yoghurt and margarine containers marked
      1, 2, 3, 4, 5 and R;
  Empty and dry paint tins.
Unacceptable items:
  Plastic bags;
  Vegetation;
  Ceramics and porcelain;
  Broken glass;
  Pyrex cookware;
  Mirrors or windows;
  Light globes or tubes;
  Plastic toys and packaging;
  Polystyrene or bubble wrap;
  Ice-cream, yoghurt and margarine containers not
      marked 1, 2, 3 4, 5 and R.

*The council says it accepts dirty bottles, tins and cans but warns if they're not rinsed, they may
  attract unwanted visitors.

TIP: Set up additional recycling bins. This is particularly useful if you live in an apartment block. Have a bin with non-ferrous metals, ferrous metals and non-recyclable plastics, such as polystyrene. Recyclers will pay money for materials that councils don't accept and turn them into things like building materials and CD casings. See www.respa.org.au.

DID YOU KNOW? *Extension cords contain copper which can be recycled. In fact, you might find when appliances are left out for council clean-up, the electrical cords are cut off. The reason is you can make money from the copper.*

Pets

Australians spend a fortune on their pets. Have you ever thought about how they could make some money for you? It sounds crazy but apparently some owners use dog hair, particularly from poodles, for felting, weaving and knitting. The Hand Weavers and Spinners Guild of NSW has a tutorial with more information. There's also a book called *Knitting with Dog Hair: Better a sweater from a dog you know and love than from a sheep you'll never meet*. We just hope the sweater doesn't smell like a wet dog when it's damp!

If your pet sheds fur on your couch, put on some disposable rubber gloves and wash your gloved hands in soap and water.

Shake your hands to remove the bulk of the water, rub your hands over the couch and the fur will stick to the gloves. If your dog or cat chews the furniture, deter cats by wiping the area with mothballs, naphthalene flakes or Vicks VapoRub and deter dogs by wiping with a little lavender oil.

TIP: Save money by buying generic brand pet food.

SAVE: OLD BIRDCAGES

OTHER USES:

+ Use the birdcage to store **seedling trays**. It keeps the birds away while seeds are germinating and can be hung out of the way.
+ Put them in the **children's toy box**. They can become toy car garages or doll's houses.

TIP: When cleaning out the budgie cage, place it in an area in the garden that needs fertilising. Bird poo is great for the garden.

CHANGE FOR GOOD: Two Australians now living in the US want to draw attention to the effect of global warming on the Great Barrier Reef and are doing so by crocheting, with dozens of crochet enthusiasts, a colourful wool 3000-square foot replica of the reef.

How to repair flyscreens

As outlined in *How to be Comfy*, it's best to completely replace rather than repair flyscreen, but if it's a small hole and you want to repair it, you can make a patch. Cut a square of matching flyscreen and place it over the damaged area. Either sew a running stitch around the square with matching poly-cotton thread or apply craft glue to the edges to keep it in place.

To replace flyscreen in an aluminium frame, buy flyscreen 1½cm larger than the edge of the frame. You'll notice there's a plastic lining in the groove between the edge of the frame and the wire. This is called beading, or PVC spline. Remove this with a screwdriver. Then remove the old or damaged flywire and place the new flywire over the area. Replace the plastic beading using a screwdriver to work it back into place, making sure that the flywire is evenly stretched across the frame as you go. Then use a beading wheel or spline roller (available at hardware stores) to roll the bead in. Cut off excess wire with a sharp knife or scissors.

WHY IT MATTERS: Bees are disappearing in the United States. Beekeepers in 24 states have reported losses of 30–60 per cent on the west coast and, in some cases, more than 70 per cent on the east coast and in Texas. Scientists are testing several theories including stress, toxins and viruses introduced by bees brought in from other countries. Bees pollinate more than $14 billion of US seeds and crops a year.

The pool/spa

Backyard pools can be lots of fun but they also use a lot of water and energy. Make your pool more environmentally friendly and reduce evaporation by using a cover. A cover will also help you save money on pool chemicals because UV light breaks chlorine down. The more sunny days there are, the more chlorine you'll need to use. Using a cover also means less algae production because it needs sun to grow. If your pool filter works efficiently, you'll need fewer chemicals to keep the pool clean. Check for leaks regularly so you don't waste water. And don't have the water level so high that water splashes out every time someone splashes in. Save your backwashing until there's been lots of rain so you won't have to refill your pool from the tap. Consider heating the pool with solar power and top up the water from a rainwater tank. Check with your local council for more information on pools and spas.

DID YOU KNOW? *The average backyard swimming pool needs 50,000 litres of water to fill it.*

SAVE: SWIMMING CAPS

OTHER USES:

+ Unless they have perished, cut old swimming caps into **elastic bands**.
+ Use them for **grip** when opening tight jars and lids.

TIP: Don't leave items made of rubber in the sun because they will perish more quickly. To prevent perishing, rub with talcum powder after cleaning. If rubber has started to perish, rub with coarse salt which acts like a sander and removes the perished material.

The shed

Whether your shed is big enough to hold a workshop or only small with a few shelves, it's a perfect space to store all those household items you've saved ready to reuse! Just make sure you have a sense of organisation or you won't be able to find what you need when you need it. One idea is to place masking tape along shelves and write in marker pen what's above.

Lawn-mowers

You might be surprised to learn that a typical 4-stroke lawn-mower produces as much pollution in one hour as four cars. If you have only a small area of lawn it's far better for the planet to use a push mower rather than an electric or petrol one. Shannon thinks the best mower is named Nick, her professional lawn-mower! If you have a petrol lawn-mower, reduce emissions by keeping the fuel mix at the correct level. If there's black smoke coming from the mower, there's too much oil in the mix. White smoke means there's too little oil in the mix. And when you're mowing the lawn, don't cut the grass too short or you'll have increased water evaporation which may cause dieback. Use the cut grass as mulch or add it to your compost.

TIP: Donate old lawn-mowers or take them to a scrap-metal recycler.

SAVE: OUTSIDE BROOMS

OTHER USES:

+ Add the handle to **anything that needs to be extended**.
+ The handle is a great **plant support, wardrobe hanger or curtain rod**.
+ Make your own **boot scraper** from an old broom head. See page 12 in *How to be Comfy* for details.
+ Turn the handle into a **toilet roll holder**. Fill a small

terracotta pot with sand, place the broom handle in the middle and stack your spare toilet rolls on top.

+ Use the handle for **cleaning** and getting into tight corners, such as skirting boards, where a broom can't reach. Sharpen one end with a utility knife, wrap in fabric and secure with an elastic band.

+ Make your own **lagerphone** (like The Bushwackers). Loosely nail beer bottle tops all over a broom handle and thump it on the ground.

SAVE: OLD LADDERS

OTHER USES:

+ Use ladders as **racks**. Place them in the rafters of the garage and hang tools from the rungs.

+ Create a country-style kitchen! Suspend a ladder from the ceiling and **hang pots and pans** from it. If the ceiling is too high, put the ladder on a hoist so you can raise or lower it as needed.

+ Prop a ladder against a wall or at the end of a bedroom wardrobe to **hang scarves, belts and other accessories**.

+ Paint with waterproof paint and use as a **towel rack** in the bathroom.

+ Paint an old stepladder to coordinate with the kitchen, place it in a corner and use it to **store pots and pans**.

+ Use a stepladder in the garden to display **pot plants**.

SAVE: OLD PUSHBIKES

OTHER USES:

+ If a bike is broken, take it to a bike shop so that they can **reuse the parts**.
+ When Shannon lived in the country, she converted a pushbike so it could **power a generator**. The wheel at the back of the bike was removed, it sat on a stand, the chain was attached to the front of the generator to turn it and when someone furiously pedalled, the generator charged the batteries.

TIP: Goodwillbicycles.com collects old bikes and gives them to disadvantaged communities. More than 7000 bikes have been shipped to East Timor.

SAVE: OLD WETSUITS

OTHER USES:

+ Turn them into **wine bottle holders**. Trim to size, sew around the edge and cut out a hole to make a handle.
+ Make into a protective **laptop computer case**.
+ Turn into **stubby holders**.

SAVE: OLD BRICKS

OTHER USES:

+ Old bricks are always handy to have around. Keep a **small stack in the shed**.
+ They're great for using as **pavers** because they're so strong.
+ Use as **garden edging**.
+ Use to **hold a gate open**.
+ If you don't want them, **recycle** them.

SAVE: OLD ROOFING TILES

OTHER USES:

+ These make great **garden edges**.
+ You can **sell** them as clean fill. You don't get much money but they're collected from your home. Consult the *Yellow Pages* or look online.

DID YOU KNOW? *To save fuel costs and reduce carbon emissions, Scandinavian airline SAS is flying more slowly. The airline has reduced the cruising speed of its planes from 860 kilometres per hour to 780 kilometres per hour. A flight between Oslo and London takes about 10 minutes longer. The company says it's saved millions.*

The garage

Although designed to house a car, many people use their garage for storage. As with the shed, you need good organisation or you won't be able to find things when you need them. Either recycle bookshelves to store things or buy cheap shelving from the hardware store. Use masking tape along the shelf and mark what's being stored. To protect items, box them in old fruit boxes and add a cover or use shoe boxes. Spray with surface spray to deter nasties. Old drawers are also handy to use for storage.

Cars

Cars add significantly to greenhouse gases and account for about one-third of household emissions. As petrol prices continue to rise many households are buying smaller, hybrid cars and using more public transport. There are things you can do right now to reduce your car use. Before getting into the car, ask yourself if you could walk, ride a bike or take the bus. When driving, think about being more fuel efficient. Don't spend too much time warming the car up, modern cars only need thirty seconds to get warm, ease your pedal from the metal and keep a consistent speed because rapid acceleration and deceleration uses more petrol. Don't carry around more weight in the car than you need, so remove roof racks and ski racks when you don't need them. And don't overuse the air conditioning: it can increase fuel consumption by 10 per cent.

There's not much you can do about the price of petrol at the bowser but one way to save money is to be aware of the fuel price cycle at service stations.

You can also save money and do your bit to help the environment if your car runs efficiently:

Have it serviced regularly;

Keep the tyres inflated at the optimum levels;

Check the oil;

Have any exhaust issues seen to.

Take old cars to wreckers or auto parts recyclers. It's unlikely you'll get much money but parts can be reconditioned or recycled. The Auto Parts Recyclers Association of Australia has more information at www.apraa.com including a guide on how to dispose of various auto parts. You can find out what individual parts are worth on the internet.

TIP: Car-share with neighbours, friends or colleagues or consider using a car-sharing company. There are several car-sharing companies that operate where members pay an annual fee and are charged by the hour for the use of a car. Users book a car for a certain time, pick it up and return it to a designated spot and don't have to worry about fuel, maintenance or insurance costs. Find them online.

CHANGE FOR GOOD: The US city of Denver has introduced a 'Driving Change' program to reduce greenhouse gas emissions from cars. Four hundred private vehicles will have a device installed to monitor time spent braking, idling, accelerating and speeding. The results will be posted on the internet with recommendations for reducing fuel consumption. The city hopes to reduce emissions in this way by 10 per cent.

 DID YOU KNOW? *The average six-cylinder car adds around 5 tonnes of greenhouse gas to the atmosphere each year which is enough to fill 34,750 garbage bins.*

How to wash a car using only 15 litres of water

Half fill a bucket with water and add 1 teaspoon of tea tree oil and 1 teaspoon of dishwashing liquid. Cover the head of a soft broom with a pair of old pantyhose. Dip the broom in the bucket and sweep from the back of the car to the front in parallel lines. Once you've gone over the whole car, do the same using clean water. Pour the remaining clean water over the car and wipe down with a chamois. This method won't scratch the duco and removes bug scat, road grime and resin from trees.

SAVE: OLD STREET DIRECTORIES

OTHER USES:

+ One of the best ways to reuse old street
  directories is as **wrapping paper**. Tape several
  pages together for a large present.

 DID YOU KNOW? *When the UK's chief scientific
adviser Sir David King was asked by a young woman
at a lecture what she could do to reduce greenhouse
gas emissions, his response was, 'Stop admiring
young men in Ferraris.' Ferrari owners protested
saying their sports cars produced less pollution than
four-wheel drive vehicles. King added, 'What I was
saying is you have got to admire people who are
conserving energy and not those wilfully using it.'*

SAVE: OLD TYRES

OTHER USES:

+ Use old tyres to **grow potatoes** as described on
  page 256.

How to make a tyre swing

First, make sure there's sufficient space in the yard to
swing around. Get an old tyre from your local garage
and scrub it clean with a heavy salt solution: 1 kilogram
of salt to 15-litres of water. If you have a strong tree,
find a secure branch and tie over two equal lengths of

thick hemp rope. In a narrow area, to make a swing that will go in one direction, attach the rope to two points on the tyre and secure either side to the nearest sturdy wall or fence. If you have a larger area, tie the rope through the tyre. To make the seat for a soft swing, use two (or four for adults) inner tubes and knot them through each other to make a figure of eight. Tie a rope to the other ends of the inner tubes and hang over a sturdy branch.

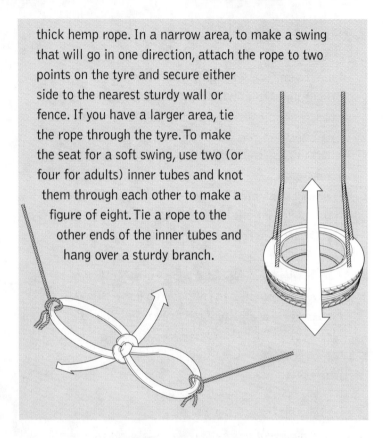

? **DID YOU KNOW?** *Old tyres can be stacked against hillsides to stop erosion and help plant regeneration.*

CHANGE FOR GOOD: A group called NetWaste is working on a scheme to recycle some of the 18 million tyres discarded each year. They hope to turn them into retaining walls, paving systems, concrete slabs and rubberised streets. See www.netwaste.org.au for more information.

TIP: Weave old seatbelts into a handbag. Jennifer's friend has a very funky gold-coloured handbag made from old seatbelts.

DID YOU KNOW? *Jet-skis are huge polluters. According to the US Environmental Protection Agency, driving a two-stroke engine jet-ski for one hour produces the same pollution as a car driven more than 100,000 miles. And then there's the noise pollution.*

DID YOU KNOW? *If you want to get involved in environmental causes there are many organisations you can join. Search online to find a group that shares your passions.*

Index

NOTES

NOTES

NOTES

NOTES

NOTES

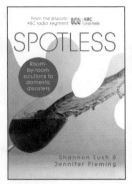

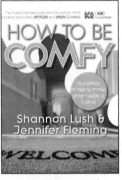